'QUOTE UNQUOTE'

'QUOTE UNQUOTE'

My top 100 Football Stories

Philip Micallef

FAIRPLAY
PUBLISHING

First published in 2022 by Fair Play Publishing
PO Box 4101, Balgowlah Heights NSW 2093 Australia
www.fairplaypublishing.com.au

ISBN: 978-1-925914-36-8

ISBN: 978-1-925914-37-5 (ePub)

© Philip Micallef 2022

The moral rights of the authors have been asserted.

Thank you to News Limited and SBS for permission to reproduce the material originally written for their print and online publications.

All rights reserved. Except as permitted under the *Australian Copyright Act 1968* (for example, a fair dealing for the purposes of study, research, criticism or review), no part of this book may be reproduced, stored in a retrieval system, communicated or transmitted in any form or by any means without prior written permission from the Publisher.

Photos: Alamy, PA, Fair Play Collection
Cover design and typesetting by Leslie Priestley.

All inquiries should be made to the Publisher via sales@fairplaypublishing.com.au

A catalogue record of this book is available from the National Library of Australia.

Contents

Introduction	vi
The National Team	1
The Global Scene	60
The A-League	87
The Big Interviews	128
The Socceroos Greats	146
The Obituaries	172
The Top Brass	182
About the Author	199

Introduction

When I pulled up stumps on my career as a professional journalist in 2021, I realised I had come to a stage in my life when I needed something to do.

Since gardening is not my thing, I welcomed Fair Play Publishing's offer to record some of my best and most significant media contributions in the form of a book.

The 100 curated stories presented in *Quote, Unquote* are a minuscule representation of the highs and lows of the game in Australia and abroad since I arrived in this vast country in 1981 from that little rock in the middle of the Mediterranean called Malta.

The articles are designed to capture the prevailing mood of the football fraternity over the years as the world game sought to gain acceptance within a difficult, unforgiving and often hostile Australian environment.

The collection of edited stories that appeared in the *Daily Telegraph* and *Sunday Telegraph* newspapers and *The World Game* website is divided into seven segments.

It comprises the Socceroos, the global game, the A-League, the big-name interviews, the 'Socceroos Greats', the obituaries and the administration.

It is a potted and subjective history of the game—by no means complete—as seen by an ordinary fan, which is essentially what I have always been and will always be.

Quote, Unquote is basically a trip down memory lane, if you like.

I wish to thank the publisher for offering me the chance to 'tell my side of the football story' that was a big part of my life for decades.

I also would like to offer my gratitude to former employers ©SBS and News Limited for allowing me to reproduce their material.

And last but not least I should also publicly acknowledge the support of my family during an exhilarating journey of a lifetime.

The National Team

The Socceroos are the focal point of the game in Australia and have provided hundreds of thousands of followers with moments of breathtaking exhilaration and others of abject despair.

England's EURO '96 manager Terry Venables explained why he left the home of football to take on the Socceroos job.

Telling it straight: Venables likes what he sees
4 February 1997

It all started with a phone call, quite out of the blue. An intermediary working on behalf of Soccer Australia got in touch with Terry Venables in London in late 1996.

The request was simple: Would he like to speak to chairman David Hill about coaching the Australians in their forthcoming World Cup campaign?

"David Hill rang me and said he would be coming to England in three weeks," Venables disclosed yesterday.

"He offered me the job and gave me a lot of time to think about it.

"I'm a great believer that you've got to travel around the world if you want to play world football.

"I'm always excited about the challenge of doing something new.

"I looked at the Australians who play abroad and thought we had a realistic chance of playing in the World Cup."

After thinking about Hill's offer, the man who took England to the brink of their first major honour in 30 years said to himself: Why not?

Thus started one of the most sensational stories associated with football in this country.

Over a coffee in Sydney, Venables was generous enough to give me some of his time.

What's your opinion of the Australian football scene? Coming from a fully professional background, have you been disappointed in any areas?

"Not really. Football here is not just starting as in America. You've had a league for a long time and games are drawing good crowds and the papers seem to devote more space to football.

"It's very encouraging. I was pleased with the players' performance in the four-nation series and with their attitude at training. You've also got a few go-ahead people determined to make football work."

Would you like anything changed in the way the game is run here?

"I always want things changed, even in England. I believe in experimenting in the lower leagues which may improve the game overall.

"If we get results then it will be worthwhile. In tennis you have line judges and cameras which make the game more professional. Football should look at these things. There's nothing wrong with trying."

What's your ideal way of playing football?

"Every team I've coached—whether it was Crystal Palace, Queens Park Rangers, Barcelona, Tottenham or England—some fans may have been critical of me but they never complained about the brand of football my teams have played. Of course, if opponents choose to play it tough we've got to be able to deal with that as well."

Hope I'm not being naive here but what's more important: a successful side or an entertaining one?

"Club football is a business, no doubt about that, but there's a difference. If a club makes $4m at the end of the season but gets relegated is it successful? You've got to satisfy your club and the fans."

What's your attitude towards the media in general?

"Like coaches and players you get the good and the bad. Some journalists take time out to think things through and have an unbiased opinion. Others have nothing in their mind except to sell newspapers, doing what they're told to do by some guy back at the office who does not have to go out and face people.

"It is unfortunate that some journalists' stories can get somebody out of a job. They all cry out they've got mortgages to pay but so do coaches and managers. To be honest I have not had much chance to make a judgement on Australia's sporting press. Same as in England, you're always looking for an angle."

Some people did not exactly welcome your appointment with open arms. Any complaints about the way the Aussie media has treated you?

"None at all. I'm very satisfied. But it's early days. As I go along I'll feel my way and I'll treat people the same way they treat me."

Had England beaten Germany at EURO '96, would we be talking in Sydney now?

"I don't know. England were not prepared to offer me a contract until after the end of the tournament, which was unacceptable to me.

"You just can't let the horse go and have a bet on it afterwards. You do not let managers get to the end of their contracts before offering them a new one. That's when I told them before the start of the tournament to get someone else."

It would be a delicious irony if Australia were to reach France '98 and England do not, wouldn't it?

"You're not going to get me on that one. I'd like to see England get through because I'm English and I'd like to see the Aussies get through because I'm a professional.
"I've been looking forward to moving here and I think I'm going to enjoy it. Although I must emphasise once again that reaching the World Cup is not going to be easy."

* * *

Australia's failure to beat Iran in Melbourne for a spot in the 1998 World Cup was probably the lowest point in our game's history. We were so close!

Four minutes that crushed a nation's dream
1 December 1997

It was supposed to be the crowning glory of Aussie football's revival.

Everything was right for a night to remember.

A marvellous stadium, a fantastic atmosphere, a Socceroos team playing its finest football in decades and a sympathetic media just waiting to feed the public with a memorable, feel-good story.

Then all of a sudden it went horribly wrong.

Australia were cruising. Iran were gone. Then disaster stuck.

Four minutes of madness: that's what it took for our dream of reaching the first World Cup since 1974 to be shattered.

After doing more than enough in the first hour of the game to make our bold entry to the French football feast look like a fait accompli, our world came crashing down with Iran's cruel double blow late in the game.

Eighty-five thousand distraught spectators and a vast television audience just could not comprehend how a team could play so well for so long and still crash out.

But after the most incredible and bizarre match I have had the misfortune to attend, the Australians now will have to assume the familiar role of spectators as Jamaica, the United States, Tunisia and Japan strut their stuff on the biggest stage of them all.

One can attribute our 'loss' on away goals to a lack of concentration from the back three that let Iran off the hook.

One also wonders whether Terry Venables was right in picking Steve Horvat in the key sweeper's role instead of experienced and accomplished Milan Ivanovic.

But the point is a gross miscarriage of justice was carried out at the MCG on Saturday.

Australia were the better team over the two legs that drew almost a quarter of a million spectators and they deserved to qualify.

It is hard to tell how long it would take Australian football to pick itself up from such a devastating debacle.

The fallout could see the end of chairman David Hill.

Even Venables's position is tenuous now that he has failed to steer Australia into the finals.

Which is unfortunate.

Today we should have been celebrating one of the greatest moments not only in Australian football but in the country's sport.

Being such a small nation with a population of a mere 18 million that regularly churns out champions in most sporting spheres, we should have been showing the world we can also do it in the greatest sport.

But it was not to be. The 2002 World Cup seems an eternity away now.

* * *

After the Socceroos failed to reach the 1998 World Cup the position of coach Terry Venables came under the microscope. Public opinion was divided.

Should we retain Terry Venables?
22 February 1998

There are three key questions we need to ask when arguing the case for or against Terry Venables. Is he a good coach? Did he make the Socceroos a better team? And do we still need him?

The answers are: of course he is, absolutely and yes, if we can give him something to do.

One can so easily dismiss Venables as a flop after his failure to get the Socceroos to the World Cup in France. But that would be a cop-out, a knee-jerk reaction.

The reason we did not qualify has nothing to do with Tel. The MCG result was either a travesty of justice or else we plainly were not good enough. Or both.

As Australian football tries to come to terms with the Melbourne debacle, it should be clever enough to build on the positives that have emerged from Tel's era and not dwell on the negatives.

Football has done too little of the former and too much of the latter over the years. It's not the way to go.

Tel's coaching skills are indisputable. Just ask any Socceroos squad member.

Curiously, his managerial career has been punctuated by spectacular failures.

Such as when hot favourites Barcelona lost the 1986 European Cup final to Steaua Bucharest or when England lost the 1996 European Championship semi-final to Germany or when four minutes of madness against Iran in November cost Australia a spot in the 1998 World Cup.

But on each occasion the teams for which Venables was responsible were a huge improvement on the ones he had inherited.

Coaches are sometimes given too much credit for what players do on the field. Similarly they can be unfairly blamed.

Let's be honest. It was not Tel's fault that Barca missed all their kicks in a penalty shootout. It was not his fault that Darren Anderton squandered a sitter that would have given England a golden-goal victory and it surely was not his fault that Hungarian referee Sandor Puhl gave Iran a lifeline by allowing a goal that was clearly offside.

But the buck stops with the coach and he accepts this.

The anti-Venables brigade wasted no time in pointing their collective finger at the Londoner.

Why didn't he pick Milan Ivanovic? Why did he use so many out-of-touch 'foreign' players? Why didn't we defend our two-goal lead?

It's easy to be wise after the event.

Sweeper Steve Horvat had not put a foot wrong before allowing Khodadad Azizi through for the killer equaliser. And nobody had criticised Horvat's selection before the match, anyway.

The reason Tel picked so many foreign-based stars who were not playing regularly for their clubs was because, with respect, they were still more gifted and far more experienced than the best of our very modest national league.

Again, no prior argument over Tel's selections.

Tel might have erred on only one count at the MCG. He should have made sure our midfielders stifled any flickering resistance left in the outclassed Iranians.

Perhaps it was his cocky nature or English background that proved his doing. You know, winning in style and all that. Fancy an Italian or German coach going for the jugular at two goals up.

To his credit, unlike many of his Socceroos predecessors, Tel took defeat on the chin and never once complained about bad refereeing or rotten luck which of course he was perfectly entitled to.

Few people seem to want to remember that this Australian team has become pretty hard to beat and pretty good to watch.

Aussie sports fans like their players and teams to have a go and in Tel's Roos they saw a cavalier side that was prepared to play a modern, all-purpose type of attacking football.

No more seven-man defences, isolated strikers and hope-for-the-best tactics.

This fresh mentality was no more evident than in the games with Hungary in Budapest, Tunisia in Tunis, Iran in Melbourne and Brazil in Riyadh. Australia had never played better football.

Some point out that Tel would have been instantly sacked if he were coach of England, Italy, Germany or Brazil and failed to take them to the World Cup.

These are well-established football countries that have no time for failure.

We are luckier in a way. We are relative rookies and we must be patient.

We've got to look at the future because our time will come if we keep improving.

So if Venables is still available to Australian football and is prepared to spend more time here we should do everything possible to keep him in some capacity.

I never thought that being based in London was ever as big a problem as some made it out to be because the bulk of our players play abroad anyway.

Now that we have nothing much to look forward to, Tel could still be an asset to Australia if he can impart his vast experience on our coaches.

If that is what he wants to do, that is.

Unfortunately, it appears Tel might not come back when his contract expires in July. Which is a shame.

Yet if Australian football makes Tel's high standards a benchmark for success, then some good might come from that wretched night in Melbourne.

* * *

Australian superstar Harry Kewell carried the bulk of the fans' expectations surrounding the 2002 World Cup playoff with Uruguay.

Time for Kewell to deliver for Australia
20 November 2001

D-Day has arrived for Harry Kewell, Australia's great white hope in the World Cup showdown with Uruguay at the MCG tonight.

The Socceroos face the two-time world champions in the first game of a two-leg playoff for the right to play in the 2002 finals.

And the smiling assassin with the choirboy looks, who has mesmerised Europe with his extraordinary exploits for Leeds United, is now expected to give something back to the country that gave him the opportunity to become a genuine superstar and a millionaire at 23.

Kewell, who was raised in Sydney's western suburbs, has not always put country before club as he rightly sought to cement his place in the cut-throat world of England's Premier League.

He has donned the Socceroos jersey only 10 times.

He often said he was never interested in 'Mickey Mouse' games and would only play for the Australian team in the matches that mattered.

Well, tonight's match is one that matters. Big time.

Not just for him. Or the Socceroos who dream of playing in football's biggest party. Or Frank Farina who is planning the biggest coup of his coaching career.

The match is vital for a maligned sport hell-bent on gaining acceptance in a land of Aussie rules, rugby league, rugby union and cricket.

Kewell is one of Europe's finest footballers and has the uncanny ability to turn matches on his own.

After weaving his special brand of magic for his club, we now hope he does the same thing for his country.

* * *

A shock loss to New Zealand in the 2002 Oceania Nations Cup did not go down well with the football family. The natives became very restless.

Shocker Australia must move with the times
20 July 2002

Socceroos coach Frank Farina must love his job dearly.

How else would one explain his refusal to tell his fumbling employers at Shocker Australia to stick the position and walk away to greener and saner pastures.

After yet another international fiasco—this time against our neighbours from New Zealand in the Oceania Nations Cup final—recriminations are flying in all directions.

Our stay-away stars are accused of lacking patriotism while Farina says his depleted team was ill-prepared for an international tournament.

New Soccer Australia chairman Ian Knop reckons Farina should stop complaining and accept responsibility for the humbling 1–0 defeat.

Knop says we should be able to beat teams like New Zealand, anyway.

What narrow-mindedness, what arrogance, what stupidity.

Knop fails to concede that the series took place at the wrong time and for a while we were not sure if he could afford to send a team to be sacrificed in Auckland.

This after declaring that selected players would have to forfeit their holidays and play for nothing.

The reason our stars did not give Knop the reply any professional sportsman would give to such an insulting proposal was because Farina was sensible enough not to select the 'foreigners'.

Farina, a young coach who is learning to juggle the demands of high-profile footballers with those of his national team, has always adopted the attitude of keeping the peace as long as he gets his main men for the matches that matter.

Which is fair enough. But he may have to change his attitude.

As last year's playoff with Uruguay showed so painfully, we cannot expect our foreign stars to gel at the push of a button.

And as the gap between Australia and the rest of Oceania continues to narrow we certainly are not strong enough to be able to dominate the region with our second-string team.

Knop was wrong to say that Farina was out of order in complaining about the substandard preparations for the Oceania series.

It was like asking Farina to climb Uluru with one foot strapped behind his body, telling him to stop complaining then berating him for not reaching the summit.

As Australian football reels from yet another debacle, the upshot of this latest shemozzle is that while Senegal, the United States, South Korea and Japan continue to boost their image on the world stage, in Australia we still argue about basic things most countries would have settled ages ago.

Some things never change.

* * *

As cash-strapped Leeds United continued their downward spiral, Socceroos striker Harry Kewell faced some tough decisions.

Kewell needs to move on from Leeds
28 March 2003

Harry Kewell, for goodness' sake, get the hell out of Leeds. There's no future for you at Elland Road.

Australia's must famous football product is having talks with Leeds about a fourth upgrade to his contract which expires at the end of next season.

Indications are that Kewell and Leeds are happy to extend their prolific partnership.

Yet Kewell, 34, might be interested to know that ultimately he would be the loser if he commits his future to the Yorkshire club.

Kewell is a born winner and deserves a more refined team than Leeds, who could be relegated in a few weeks.

Australia's golden boy should look at broadening his under-achieving career elsewhere, not necessarily in Britain.

Leeds have become the epitome of physical football and the team's aggressive style does not complement Kewell's silky skills.

People interested in Kewell's fortunes would not be surprised to learn that his game has stagnated in the last two years.

It seems Kewell, who has said he would like to become the world's greatest player, has reached a point of no return at Leeds.

At times he and some of his teammates seem to be on a different wavelength.

So his game would be enhanced if he were to play for a Manchester United, an Arsenal or any one of Europe's top clubs—teams that embrace the more technical and subtle aspects of the game.

Who knows what more magic Kewell could conjure if he were to perform with such luminaries as Beckham, Zidane, Henry, Saviola, Rivaldo or Del Piero?

Make no mistake, European interest in Kewell is real, huge and won't go away.

Kewell has lived in Yorkshire for the best part of a decade and feels at home there. Another contract with Leeds would appear to suit him and his family.

But being a professional footballer, Kewell has to decide what's best for his career.

Surely he is affluent enough not to let one or two million dollars make up his mind about where he should play.

What Kewell needs more than money is to be in the limelight. He needs to play for a winning side that tends to showcase his extraordinary skills on the biggest stage of all—the Champions League.

At the moment it looks like it's going to be a long time before Leeds even make the UEFA Cup.

Which is why Kewell must not waste away in Leeds. For his sake, Australia's sake and football's sake.

* * *

'QUOTE UNQUOTE'

Alvaro Recoba set the scene for an emotion-charged clash with his explosive comments before the World Cup playoff between Australia and Uruguay.

Recoba declares Uruguay's divine right to win
15 November 2005

Uruguayan superstar Alvaro Recoba yesterday boldly declared that his team had a divine right to play in the World Cup and Australia had no chance of getting through to the finals in Germany.

Recoba, 29, who plays his club football for Italy's Internazionale, claimed after a 75-minute training session at Aussie Stadium that the Socceroos team had gone backwards since 2001.

"I believe this Australian team is weaker than the one we faced four years ago," said the striker who played in the playoff that the South Americans won 3-1 on aggregate.

Recoba, the master craftsman they call 'El Chino' because of his oriental looks, has hit some marvellous goals in a chequered career at club and national level.

But yesterday he scored a spectacular own goal that won't be forgiven by 82,000 fans tomorrow when he announced: "We have a right to be at the World Cup.

"I'm not saying that we have to force our way into the finals but it is normal for a country like ours to be at the game's biggest event.

"The Australians obviously will try their utmost to beat us and this is only logical.

"But the fact is that Uruguay are Uruguay and the Australians should respect us for this.

"We are a big country with a rich past, a major footballing country that has won far more (than Australia).

"I do not know what type of game we can expect on Wednesday but what I am sure of is that we will get to Germany. We're a strong team and in a good position. One-nil should be enough for us."

As about 200 drum-beating, flag-waving and chanting Uruguay fans followed the training session, Recoba said it was "nice to come here so many thousands of kilometres from home and be greeted by many Uruguayans living in Australia.

"We've got to give them a night to remember," Recoba said.

Recoba is one of Uruguay's finest ever footballers and was deemed to be the main difference between the two sides when they last met in 2001 for a place in the 2002 World Cup in Korea and Japan.

Australia won the first leg 1-0 at the MCG in Melbourne but Recoba and his amigos crushed the Socceroos 3-0 in the return at the historic Centenario Stadium, which was the scene of Uruguay's first World Cup triumph in 1930.

Recoba was again in sparkling form in the first leg in Montevideo at the weekend.

It was from one of his wicked free kicks that attacking fullback Dario Rodriguez came in from the blind side of Australia's defence to head in the only goal of the match.

Recoba represents the entertaining side of Uruguayan football, which also has a sound reputation for gamesmanship and thuggery.

Only last week Brazil's World Cup hero Ronaldo warned the Australians that Uruguay would use every trick in the book to secure their ticket to Germany.

Recoba would not elaborate on the Brazilian's statement.

"I'm not saying anything," he said.

"Let's play the game on Wednesday, get to the World Cup and then we'll see."

Recoba's view on the strength of the Australian team was contradicted by his teammate Dario Silva, who said the Socceroos were an improved outfit.

* * *

The playoff between Australia and Uruguay for a spot in the 2006 World Cup was tense and tight and it came down to a penalty shootout lottery.

The shootout that obliterated 32 years of pain
17 November 2005

It's football's version of Russian roulette. The winners take all. The losers are history.

It's unfair, cruel and does not in any way reflect supremacy on the field.

It has made big superstars look very little, turned goalkeepers into all-time heroes and driven entire nations to despair.

When referee Luis Medina Cantalejo blew his final whistle after 90 minutes of pulsating play plus another 30 heart-stopping minutes of extra time to signal the start of the dreaded shootout, no one in their right mind would have put any money on the Socceroos, who have a history of World Cup disasters.

After failing to qualify for a World Cup for 32 years how could we possibly go through via a shootout against such an experienced side?

The omens were not good.

But as soon as Harry Kewell came forward to take the first kick, right above him a full moon came out from behind a cloud to guide his competent shot past Uruguay's goalkeeper Fabian Carini.

But perhaps it was not a bright full moon that was casting a benevolent smile on the Socceroos.

It could have been Johnny Warren himself who was guiding his beloved Green and Gold to the game's heavenly event—the World Cup.

With 82,000 fans desperately baying for Uruguayan blood, Dario Rodriguez stepped up in reply but super keeper Mark Schwarzer threw himself sideways to block his tentative effort.

A cool Lucas Neill made it 2–0 to put the Socceroos in control of the shootout.

With tension rising, Gustavo Varela made up for a miserable game by pulling one back for Uruguay.

However, Tony Vidmar, with years of experience behind him, nonchalantly slotted home the third shot before Fabian Estoyanoff again narrowed the margin for the visitors.

After three kicks each the Australians were 3–2 up and looking good. Germany was getting closer.

Up stepped captain Mark Viduka—surely the man to carry the Socceroos home when under pressure.

But there was further drama to come because the big man had the fans' hearts in their mouths when he stumbled on his run-in and hit a timid shot wide of the post.

Uruguay, however, incredibly failed to take advantage because Marcelo Zalayeta's shot was parried by a diving Schwarzer.

John Aloisi then stepped up to the spot with the weight of an entire nation's expectations on his shoulders.

Uruguay keeper Carini picked right, got a touch but, unlike Schwarzer, he could not stop the ball from going in.

The goal sealed the Socceroos' victory and their ticket to world football's grand event in Germany next June, 32 years after they played in their first and last tournament in the same country.

The stadium and indeed the whole of Australia erupted in celebration.

It was the second time that Schwarzer had covered himself in glory in a World Cup shootout in Sydney.

In 1993 at the Sydney Football Stadium, he was the hero of Australia's victory over Canada that took the Aussies to a final playoff against Argentina, which they lost 2–1 on aggregate.

That defeat, and all the others since 1974, looked a million miles away last night.

Uruguay may well have felt they had a divine right to play in the World Cup but the Australians—via Schwarzer—seemed to have the hand of God to help them end many years of World Cup heartbreak.

For Uruguay it was the most cruel way to lose after two draining, high-pressure matches in four days.

But for Australia it was the most exhilarating way to win.

* * *

With the 2006 World Cup less than three months away, Japan coach Zico gave his views on the forthcoming clash with Australia during a candid chat in Tokyo.

We're out to get you, warns Japan boss Zico
28 March 2006

Arthur Antunes Coimbra, who the sporting world knows as Zico, is a hopeless football romantic.

As a key member of that magnificent Brazil side of 1982 that is probably the finest team never to win a World Cup, Zico ideally would like his players to master the art of his native 'jogo bonito', the beautiful game.

Zico firmly believes that miracles are still very much part and parcel of the modern game and he is hoping for one in a few months.

He speaks very good Italian with a few Portuguese words thrown in but his Brazilian droll is unmistakable.

He comes across as a warm and relaxed man who is settling in for a chat about the game that made him famous.

Yet mention the word 'Australia' and the man they call 'O Galo' (The Rooster) perks up.

When asked to discuss Japan's first match in the World Cup against the Socceroos, Zico the romantic becomes Zico the pragmatic.

In one of the 10 conference rooms the Japanese Football Association and the J.League have at their disposal at the game's massive headquarters in downtown Tokyo, Zico did not mince his words.

"It's the decisive game in our group," he said.

"It's a game we have to win because victory would give us the right frame of mind to face Croatia and Brazil.

"We just cannot afford to lose against Australia. A draw would not be the end of the world but we will be going for a win. We have to.

"Firstly because if we lose our first game we would have to win our next one at all costs. And secondly you know that if you lose the second game you are out of the tournament after a week."

Zico said he had the highest regard for Socceroos coach Guus Hiddink.

"Australia's team are nicely set up on the field and of course this is all credit to Hiddink," he said.

"Like all other teams, the Australians have their weak points and their strong points. We must know how to play to Australia's weaknesses. The match is very important for both teams. Whoever loses is basically out."

Zico, whose Japan team minus its 'foreign' stars meet Ecuador in a trial match in Oita on Thursday, expressed surprise at the great improvement by our national team.

"The first time I played against Australia was in the mid-80s when I was playing for Udinese in Italy," he recalled.

"To be honest the level of your team was not very high then.

"But when I watched them play against Argentina in the two-leg playoff for the 1994 World Cup I thought the physical side of their game had improved considerably.

"And now of course with players like Kewell, Cahill, Bresciano, Viduka and Aloisi the Socceroos have also improved from the technical side.

"The team today is in good shape and whoever says that the Socceroos are not a strong side must have a poor appreciation of the game."

Zico said Brazil were hot favourites to win Group F at the World Cup and the remaining spot was up for grabs.

"On paper it appears the section will pan out as an even three-way fight between us, Australia and Croatia for a place in the last 16 behind Brazil," he said.

"However, on the field things can be very different.

"The pressure on Brazil is enormous and some of their stars are not in the best condition and we will have to wait and see what shape they will be in come June.

"And if you start well and things go against them you just never know in football."

So how do you stop Brazil?

"There is not much you can do except hope to catch them on an off day," Zico said.

"But if you sit back you'd be asking for trouble.

"You should pressurise their defence and not let them get into their usual pattern and rhythm.

"You should also be prepared to take a few risks ... football is all about taking risks ... and hoping for the best."

The World Cup is less than three months away and the JFA recently launched a slogan for its World Cup campaign called Samurai Blue.

The motto is probably designed to foster among Japan's football fraternity a spirit of aggression that was the symbol of the country's old warriors.

"Look, I really do not know whether that is the thinking behind the motto," Zico said.

"Football today is all about marketing and some things I do not fully understand.

"But I do know that Japanese footballers need to be sporting samurais if you like and play with the spirit of the old warriors.

"I like my players to be aggressive because being technically proficient is not enough.

"When you represent your country you have to play with spirit and the heart."

Coming from such a culturally advanced football country as Brazil, Zico had to overcome huge problems in Asia.

Japan in fact came as a bit of a culture shock to him.

"It is difficult for a Japanese player to change his mentality," he conceded.

"The greatest difficulty I had to overcome when I came here in 1991 was to make players realise that it was no crime to make a mistake on the field.

"Players should not be afraid to try anything.

"This is the biggest difference between a Japanese and Brazilian player.

"In Japan people are expected to do their job properly ... but football is different.

"Players must have the courage to improvise, like the Brazilians do.

"Today my players know they will not be replaced as soon as they make a mistake so they are playing with a new tranquillity and with a freedom of expression.

"I certainly believe in their ability so why shouldn't they believe in themselves."

The Japanese have made great strides forward in the last decade and have won the last two Asian championships, which in a way makes them the region's flag bearers in Germany.

"They have to think that way," Zico said.

"Players must know their strengths and assume responsibility.

"They need to know that many fans expect a lot from them, especially since they are winners.

"Being the champions of Asia is a good responsibility to have and they should not be afraid of it."

* * *

Australia's meek capitulation in the 2007 Asian Cup, a year after performing admirably at the World Cup, drew fierce criticism from thousands of Socceroos fans.

Time for Australia to change their playing style
23 July 2007

Let's get this straight: Australia's maiden participation in the AFC Asian Cup has been an unmitigated disaster. We got our bums kicked in a big way, no question about that.

The Socceroos' delusions of grandeur were exposed as a classic case of arrogance born out of ignorance by a number of teams that showed us they can play modern, all-purpose football with a rich blend of flair, smartness, control and humility.

The cumbersome Australians unfortunately had none of these qualities as they stumbled from one mishap to another before crashing in the quarter-finals.

Asia has been a reality check for our football and we found out to our cost that in many facets of the game we are well behind time. The World Cup in Germany seems a million years away now.

"The Asian Cup has been a learning experience for Australia," Korea Republic's Dutch coach Pim Verbeek told me in Kuala Lumpur after his side had knocked out Iran on penalties to reach the semi-finals.

"And if you think conditions at the Asian Cup were hard, wait until you have to play teams like Uzbekistan where an away match means a 20-hour trip each way. Mark my words, Asian football is not easy."

This is not a complaint about Graham Arnold, Mark Viduka or Harry Kewell or whoever was involved in this Asian pipe dream. This is all about our football culture centred on an antiquated Anglicised mentality that has not moved ahead like the rest of the world has.

Australia can justifiably claim that the conditions at the Asian Cup were not conducive to enterprising football, that they showed at times against Thailand that they were capable of putting on some decent stuff and that they went out of the tournament only on penalties to holders Japan after playing for almost an hour with 10 men following Vinnie Grella's harsh expulsion.

But to dwell on these matters is to miss the point, which is that Australia's stars were found wanting when it came to pure skills and tactics. The Socceroos were simply outplayed by three of the four teams they met.

Oman never deserved to be pegged back by Tim Cahill's late equalising goal, Iraq gave us a lesson in football technique and Japan were the better team even before Grella's red card.

So why did the same players who have made headway in some of the world's toughest leagues and put on such a fine show at the 2006 World Cup fail to leave their mark on Asian football?

Perhaps our stars cannot express themselves to the best of their ability in the green and gold jersey because they are bogged down by an old-fashioned system that turns them from artists into artisans and has more to do with physique than technique.

If Australia is smart enough it should take a good look at itself and the way it plays its football ... which is a poor man's English game that at best is simply naive and inadequate for modern times and at worst predictable, rugged and ugly.

Asia is going to be a huge challenge for Australia in the next few years but our 'English' approach to football will get us nowhere because it is not the way to go in this day and age. Nobody else plays that way anymore.

English football realised this long ago after a failure too many and the unimaginative, long-ball game is history as far as the national team is concerned.

One might argue that there would be absolutely nothing wrong with the Australian game if it reaches the same level of English football.

But England is a giant of the world game and has a much bigger population than ours and can produce far more quality players.

So it could afford to be reluctant to change its one-dimensional ways because it knew that generally it had enough stars to turn a match in a split second.

Australia does not have this luxury yet it still persists with an essentially physical game designed to stifle the life out of the opposition.

This is why we should take a leaf out of Guus Hiddink's style and try to adopt his ways right down to grassroots level.

It's either that or our historic entry into the AFC will have achieved nothing. We might as well have stayed in Oceania.

*   *   *

The Matildas turned a few heads when they reached the quarter-finals of the Women's World Cup in 2007. Their feat would be the start of bigger and better things to come.

How the 'iron ladies' stole our hearts
24 September 2007

The only other time the Matildas players made headlines in Australia was when they took off their clothes for a publicity stunt.

This time they have stunned the country by what they can do with their gear on.

Australian football's poor relations caused a stir in late 1999 when a Melbourne-based entrepreneur got them to pose naked for a calendar that sold faster than seafood on Christmas Eve.

The little known Matildas wanted instant fame and it worked a treat.

The current Matildas are more likely to leave a lasting legacy on Australia's sporting landscape after coming from nowhere to reach the quarter-finals of the 2007

'QUOTE UNQUOTE'

Women's World Cup.

The fairytale came to an end when they fell 3–2 to Brazil in Tianjin on Sunday night.

The Matildas fought valiantly against a more gifted side but could do nothing to stop a screamer from Cristiane that even the great Ronaldinho would have been proud of.

The Australians' tremendous achievements in China took us all by surprise.

However, what really captured the imagination of the public and media bang in the middle of the AFL and NRL finals was the stoic defiance shown by coach Tom Sermanni's iron ladies.

The Matildas waltzed into the FIFA tournament as rank outsiders.

They had never won a World Cup finals match but they broke the ice with a 4–1 victory over Ghana first up.

Then came the harder games against Norway and Canada in which the Australian maidens seemed to be down and out on more than one occasion.

But they managed to survive thanks to the sort of dogged resistance you would usually expect from their more illustrious Socceroos counterparts.

When all seemed lost against the highly rated Norwegians in their second match they drew level with a late, late goal from super sub Lisa De Vanna to earn a 1–1 draw.

And in their last group match with the Canadians they fell behind twice before stealing a 2–2 draw with a last-gasp goal a la Tim Cahill from experienced Cheryl Salisbury.

Flamboyant Brazil would have been frustrated by the Aussies' stubborn refusal to lie down after they had gone two goals down and lost captain Salisbury to injury early in the game.

The 33-year-old defender is a motivational speaker when she is not playing football. She might let a video of the Matildas' matches in this World Cup do all the talking for her from now on.

So where will the Matildas go from here? Will their extraordinary feats in China dispel mainstream Australia's scepticism towards the women's game?

It remains to be seen if this sudden surge of interest in the Matildas is just our way of hailing—albeit fleetingly—any national team that competes well on the international front or further proof that our new football is soaring at all levels and gaining a wider acceptance from mainstream Australia.

There is no doubt that the standard of women's football worldwide is rising and becoming more watchable but if the truth be told there still is a chasm in quality between the male and female game: much wider, perhaps, than that of men and women's tennis, golf or cricket.

If the football seen at the Women's World Cup in China was produced by men, many fans would have been entitled to feel disappointed.

And this is not being churlish—chauvinistic even—but brutally honest.

However, sport is not only about extravagantly gifted stars and the obscene megabucks they make.

Sport is mostly about sportsmen or women meeting challenges and overcoming adversity.

It is about a bunch of ambitious players like the Matildas—who are not professionals and some do not even have a job—who dared to dream and who made considerable personal sacrifices in their pursuit of glory for themselves and their country.

This is why the Aussie girls' magnificent efforts should be roundly commended, regardless of whether you like football, or more particularly, the women's version.

The women's game can never and will never be on a par with its male counterpart in terms of appeal and standard but the Matildas are no 'lesser Socceroos'.

The De Vannas and McCallums might not play the game as expertly as the Cahills and Brescianos but they should be treated with no less admiration, respect and gratitude.

The Matildas' feats on the world stage have ensured that women's football will never be the same from now on.

And they did this without the help of naked calendars.

*   *   *

Lucas Neill was the driving force behind Australia's bid to reach the 2010 World Cup. The Socceroos captain told me how much the group appreciated the fans' support, especially in away matches.

Skipper Neill leads by example
2 October 2008

As the Socceroos were walking off the field after beating Uzbekistan 1–0 in Tashkent two weeks ago, captain Lucas Neill beckoned his troops to come back: the job was not done yet because there was still some important business to attend to.

Neill, who had just played a blinder in the centre of defence, led his players to the far end of the field so they could acknowledge the strong support given to them by a small band of intrepid Aussie fans who had made the long and costly journey from Australia to support their heroes in a tough World Cup qualifier.

Neill shook hands with as many fans as possible and even took off his gold jersey and gave it to one of the supporters.

This beautiful, poignant moment showed how keen Neill's Socceroos are on forging closer links with their supporters, especially those loyal fans who follow them through thick and thin to the far corners of the world.

The mild perception that the present-day Socceroos are a bunch of pampered millionaires who ply their trade in the biggest leagues in Europe and live in a world of their own was knocked on its head by Neill's effort to make the fans know that the team was grateful for their strong backing.

This was no orchestrated PR exercise but a genuine, goodwill gesture that blew away the fans.

"As a captain I take the lead by making the guys go over to the fans," Neill, 30, said.

"And if I go over to the fans to thank them I expect my players to follow me.

"It's a natural thing that I do. The boys and I appreciated the fact that these people had come all the way from Australia to Tashkent to support us in such an intimidating environment.

"We certainly noted them on the pitch and the least we could do was go over and clap them and just say 'thank you' and maybe throw a few shirts at the crowd.

"I'm not the only person who thinks like this. We like to make the fans know that we appreciate their support, especially in away matches.

"We realise that the people in the crowd are also proud to be Australian and they always come along, sing the anthem with their Aussie shirts, and they wear them even in places where you'd think it might be a bit dangerous to wear the shirt.

"I never forget that and the rest of my team never forgets that. This is the message we are trying to give to the fans: we know how proud they are of being Australian, we know how good and privileged we are to be playing for Australia, and we appreciate them as much as they appreciate us.

"The fans do not get to see us that often but, you know, we are different to the guys they see on television.

"As the guys on TV we are concentrating and focused on what we have to do to win.

"But when we're off the pitch we are one of the nicest and most humble squads I have ever been part of and we're all so proud to be Australian."

Neill, who hails from Sydney's northern beaches, left Australia in 1995 as a 17-year-old AIS graduate to try his luck in English football. He signed professional terms for Millwall and from then on his career took off.

After six years in east London he joined Blackburn Rovers in the Premier League where he spent six successful seasons before returning to London in 2007 to join ambitious West Ham United, where he is now captain.

But Neill never forgets his roots and on Australia Day last January he made a short trip across London to the Walkabout pub in The Embankment to enjoy the day with a few hundred Aussie revellers.

"It wasn't planned," he said, almost apologetically.

"I had just finished training and I wanted to go there with my brother and some friends to celebrate Australia Day with Australian people.

"And when I went I realised how proud a nation we are. Everyone had green and gold face paint or jerseys. It was as if I had just walked into Australia."

Neill was overwhelmed and could not help himself: he put his credit card on the bar and shouted the whole place.

"They were not pestering me. All they wanted was to shake my hand, pat me on the back, have a little chat and get a photo with me," he said.

"I said to myself 'I know these guys, they earn Australian dollars and spend English pounds and sometimes it's tough'. It was a humbling experience and the least I could do was buy them a drink.

"They didn't treat me like a star but just as an Aussie. Which is the way it should be."

Neill, a private and reserved person whose dislike of the spotlight is often mistaken for aloofness, does a lot of work for the game that often goes unpublished.

He has launched the Lucas Neill Foundation, a Sydney-based scholarship designed to help young players gain first-hand experience of what's required to become a professional player.

* * *

Dutchman Pim Verbeek gave me a rare insight into his managerial methods as he and the Socceroos fought for a spot in the 2010 World Cup in South Africa.

Verbeek reveals his ruthless ways

4 October 2008

Socceroos coach Pim Verbeek is emerging as the clinical operator with the merciless methods designed to take Australia to the 2010 World Cup.

Verbeek, 52, was appointed by Football Federation Australia in late 2007 with a simple and clear job description: to get Australia to the finals in South Africa.

His contract, believed to be worth $2 million, will expire the moment our involvement in 2010 ends.

The affable Dutchman is preparing for Australia's next qualifier against Qatar in

Brisbane on October 15 but behind his relaxed and polite exterior lies a determined man who will go to great lengths to realise his ambition, leaving nothing to chance and making sure he's got all his bases covered.

He has dumped Mark Milligan from his World Cup squad because the defender has no club and has warned David Carney and Mile Sterjovski he would drop them too if they failed to play regularly for their clubs.

He picks massive squads at considerable cost as insurance for last-minute injuries and makes no apologies for adopting safety-first tactics when playing away.

With so much at stake, he plays his cards to his chest, does not give anything away and takes nothing for granted.

"That's my job, I'm thinking all the time when I am in camp of how's the best way to win a match," he said.

"I'm thinking how I can make my players be mentally 100 per cent and mislead the opposition by giving the wrong information, too much information or no information at all.

"That's the way you have to do it in international football because every detail counts and it could be the difference between winning and losing.

"I see that Qatar's new coach Bruno Metsu is already playing mind games and saying that my team is favourite to win the match.

"He's playing the underdogs game. I cannot do that because I think he's right: we are the best team in the group."

Verbeek's meticulous approach to a football match was underlined last month when Australia faced Uzbekistan in the World Cup qualifier in Tashkent.

On the eve of the match he was talking about how he planned to play it cautiously in the beginning and hope that the impatient Uzbek fans become frustrated and get on their players' backs if the score was still goalless after 20 minutes or so, forcing the home team to take a few risks and play into Australia's hands.

Verbeek later asked me not to mention the bit about the crowd getting agitated because his quotes on *The World Game* website, he said, could be picked up by local journalists who could spark a hostile fan reaction at the Pakhtakor Stadium.

"I did not want to give the Uzbeks the chance to say 'Okay, if that's what he wants ... '" Verbeek explained.

"You have to work on your opponents' weak points.

"They were already under pressure (after losing 3–0 to Qatar) and we wanted to take advantage of that. So why alert them (to our way of thinking) and make them any wiser and more determined than necessary?"

A few weeks ago he also knocked back an offer to give his views on Australia's four group adversaries.

"Why should I let my rivals know how much I know about them?" he declared.

Football fans were quite entitled to ask "Pim who?" when the former Korea Republic boss got the Socceroos job last year. But 10 months and a series of vital victories down the track, Verbeek seems to have won over the sceptics.

He knew he had big boots to fill when he took over from Graham Arnold, who filled in after the reign of Guus Hiddink who had taken the Socceroos to the World Cup for the first time in 32 years. But that did not worry bloody-minded Verbeek.

"It was not hard at all (to replace Guus) because I was never worried about what people thought of me," Verbeek said.

"I know what my qualities are and I know why the FFA gave me the job and what I had to do. But of course the only way to gain respect in a new job is to get results.

"When big-name coaches step into a new position it's a bit easier for them because they have more credibility.

"They say things and people believe them because if they are respectable coaches then they must know what they are talking about.

"But big names do not guarantee results. When I took the job I knew I had to adapt to the Australian mentality.

"I felt at home the moment I arrived here although I realised from the very beginning that I had to win games.

"We won our first World Cup qualifier against Qatar in Melbourne and played well so that made life a lot easier."

Verbeek said he was looking forward to the Qatar match that would provide the Australians with an opportunity to overtake the Group A leaders.

And he said a draw in the other group match in Saitama between Japan and Uzbekistan would make his day.

"If we beat Qatar and Uzbekistan get a result in Saitama they would put pressure on Japan in terms of qualification," he said.

"Uzbekistan are a tough side at home and the longer they are in the race the more likely they are to take points off other teams.

"Yet if they lose to Japan they might give up, which would diminish the value of our hard-fought victory in Tashkent, which was a bonus. So a draw in Japan would be perfect."

Verbeek will be keeping his fingers crossed that none of his players suffer any injuries in the weekend round of league matches in Europe and Australia.

Verbeek, who has already lost injured Aalborg defender Michael Beauchamp and will be without suspended midfielder Carl Valeri, is aware that Harry Kewell has a lingering groin injury that forced him out of Galatasaray's UEFA Cup match against Bellinzona in midweek.

The Turkish club has said that Kewell would not be allowed to travel to Australia if he can't play for them so there is a distinct possibility that the star player might not be available for the Qatar match.

"Harry is a big concern but I know what I will have to do if he does not make it, that's my job," Verbeek said.

Verbeek was asked what his Plan B was. It was a dumb question.

* * *

Argentine star Osvaldo Ardiles gave Australian football some sound advice during a visit to address a coaching conference.

Ardiles urges Australia to put the Socceroos first
17 February 2009

Argentina's World Cup legend Osvaldo Ardiles has urged Australia to make the national team the focus of its game if it is to become a genuine football power.

Ardiles, 56, was a member of the Argentine team that won the FIFA World Cup in 1978 and later forged a magnificent career with Tottenham Hotspur, where he became a cult hero.

Speaking at the end of a presentation at the Football Federation Australia Coaching Conference at Homebush, Ardiles said this was the way forward for a developing country like Australia.

"The national team has to be the top priority if Australia is to do something in world football," Ardiles said.

"I say this without any shadow of a doubt.

"Australian football is very strong and the country produces players who are fighters and have strong characters.

"But the football authorities here should now concentrate on improving the technical and tactical side of the game to take it to the next level."

The former midfielder who will be remembered for his close dribbling and slide-rule passing earlier told a packed gallery that 1978 World Cup-winning coach Cesar Luis Menotti transformed Argentine football forever.

"In 1974 Argentina was humiliated by Holland, in 1970 we did not even make it to the finals and in 1966 we fell in the second round," Ardiles said.

"We always thought we were the best in the world but come the World Cup we would not compete.

"But when Menotti took over after 1974 a transformation took place. He was a revolutionary and would become the most important person in the history of Argentine football.

"He made the national team the absolute priority of our game and made sure he had his best players available when he wanted them.

"He immediately set us a goal of winning the World Cup and he made the fans who supported their clubs with passion get behind their national team."

Ardiles played a key role in Argentina's World Cup triumph and after a superlative tournament he and squad member Ricardo Villa sensationally moved to Tottenham to become the first Argentines to play in England's old first division.

His transfer made big headlines worldwide at the time but Ardiles did not expect to take so long to adapt to the 'long ball' game played in England.

"It took me and Ricky a year and a half to get used to the English game," he said.

"For a while we felt like spectators as the ball sailed above our heads from defence to attack.

"English teams were encouraged to play the three-touch game: the goalkeeper kicks the ball upfield, somebody knocks it down and a third player puts the ball in the net.

"This was the way to play football, the clubs were told. Brazil, who won five World Cups, got it wrong.

"The only team that played good football those days were Liverpool. They could pass the ball forever and that is why they won European cups."

Ardiles said he was a great believer of the technical game, particularly the Brazilian way of playing football, and admitted "they would kill me back home if they heard me say this."

"Football is like chess," he said.

"You don't win by accident or by a loose ball. If you play good football on the ground you will eventually find an opening.

"Also, by being able to pass the ball for long periods you tend to demoralise your opponent: keep it, pass it; keep it, pass it."

Ardiles cited as an example Argentine Esteban Cambiasso's goal in the 6–0 rout of Serbia–Montenegro at the last World Cup.

The Internazionale midfielder scored one of the all-time great goals of the World Cup by slamming home Argentina's second goal at the completion of a move involving a record 24 passes.

"None of the players did anything particularly difficult, they just played simple football," Ardiles said.

"But at the end the Serbians were frustrated at not being able to get anywhere near the ball and they gave up. Any player in the world wants to touch the ball."

* * *

Mark Viduka and Harry Kewell are seen by many as Australia's finest footballers. With their best years behind them, opinion over who was the better player was divided.

Viduka and Kewell hard to split
24 March 2010

Champion forwards Mark Viduka and Harry Kewell are Australian football's finest products and their achievements across Europe have gone a long way towards giving our country the respectability it craves.

We are talking here about two knockabout Aussie blokes with Croatian and English backgrounds who emerged from the suburbs of Melbourne and Sydney to become big stars on the world stage.

Even more so than current pin-up boy Tim Cahill and before him Mark Bosnich and Craig Johnston, 'Dukes' and 'H' have left their mark on the game due to an ability to torment the world's toughest defenders with their extraordinary technique and a string of outrageous goals.

Their personalities are as different as chalk and cheese yet when they wore the all-white strip of Leeds United they were on the same wavelength and they terrorised Britain and the rest of Europe for four memorable years.

At their peak they were among the most potent and talked-about strike forces in the Premier League, if not Europe.

Viduka, 34, appears to be retired after having played no senior football with his last club Newcastle United since the end of last season while Kewell, who is three years younger, will be seeking his last big contract when his deal with Galatasaray expires at the end of the season.

So if Viduka and Kewell are regarded as Australia's finest players the burning question would have to be: who was the better player?

I believe Kewell has a wider range of attacking skills yet Viduka was stronger and a more lethal finisher. Kewell generally gave better service to the Socceroos while Viduka probably had a more rewarding club career. So my verdict, for all it's worth, is Viduka in a shootout.

Their clubs

Viduka made a name for himself as a natural striker with Melbourne Knights in the National Soccer League in the 1990s before going on an extensive tour of Europe that included stints at Croatia Zagreb (three years), Celtic (two), Leeds (four), Middlesbrough (three) and Newcastle (two).

Kewell has played for three clubs so far: Leeds (eight years), Liverpool (five) and Galatasaray (two).

Socceroos career

Viduka was picked 43 times for Australia, scoring 11 goals, while Kewell has earned 45 caps, scoring 13, with more to come. Both players took part in the 2006 World Cup.

Viduka was team captain and led the line magnificently without reward.

Kewell changed the game when he came on as a substitute in that memorable qualifier against Uruguay in 2005 and scored the late equaliser against Croatia that gave the Socceroos a spot in the round of 16.

Major honours

Viduka won three Croatian 'league and cup doubles' with Zagreb in the mid-1990s and the 2000 Scottish League Cup with Celtic. Kewell won the 2004 FA Cup and 2005 UEFA Champions League with Liverpool and the 2008 Turkish Super Cup with Gala. Both played in the Australia team that reached the 1997 Confederations Cup final against Brazil.

Technical ability

Viduka is a big, strong target man who could also move with the nimbleness of a ballet dancer and find the net from any angle with the accuracy of a sniper. He will be remembered mostly for his heading prowess, his ability to hold the ball up and his capacity to dribble in tight areas.

Kewell started as a flying left-winger who loved taking people on before supplying his forwards with tantalising crosses. He later became more proficient in the art of finishing and some of his goals for club and country defied belief.

Temperament

Viduka got an early warning of what pressures he would be under when the president of Croatia himself wanted him to leave Australia and sign for Croatia Zagreb. After three years on the Dalmatian Coast the secret was out. From that point onwards every game Viduka played would be scrutinised intensely yet he managed to forge a magnificent career despite the huge expectations placed on him by the fans and media.

Kewell too was always the subject of the highest scrutiny—especially in his five-year stint with Liverpool—mainly due to his special skills. Kewell has had his critics at home and abroad but he went about his business in his own nonchalant way, always claiming he had nothing to prove. He came back strongly when it appeared that his career was over after an injury too many in and around 2006.

Finest moments

Viduka will probably regard the four goals he scored for Leeds in a 4–3 premiership victory over Liverpool as one of the highlights of his career. He also was top scorer and player of the year in Scotland in 2000. Leading the Socceroos at the 2006 World Cup would have given him immense pride and satisfaction.

Kewell's best club days were at Leeds where he played consistently well for several years while he will fondly remember the 2–2 thriller against Croatia in Stuttgart at the 2006 World Cup when his late goal sealed Australia's qualification to the round of 16 and the sensational solo goal he scored against England in London in 2003.

Injuries

Both players, especially Kewell, have had to deal with serious injuries that would have tested their resolve and will to fight back. They both spent many months on the sidelines when they were at their peak. One wonders what they could have achieved with a bit more luck on the health front.

The question marks

Viduka would dearly have loved to score more goals for Australia than the meagre tally of 11. It was through no lack of effort and he certainly made many goals for others. Yet over the years many fans wondered why 'Dukes' was not as prolific a scorer in the green and gold jersey as he was for his distinguished clubs where he finished up with a record of a goal every two games.

Kewell has always been the Australian game's pin-up boy yet his commitment to the national team was sometimes brought into question in the days when he was trying to establish himself in English football. He, however, put all suggestions of divided loyalties to bed with some superlative performances for Australia over the years.

What Frank Farina says

Former Australia coach Frank Farina said he felt privileged to be able to work with such quality players.

"Those sorts of players come along only once in a generation, especially in a country like Australia, and to have two come through at the same time was extraordinary," he said.

"It's a shame Australia's qualifying path to the World Cup was so different prior to 2006 because they would have had three World Cups under their belts by now. Both of them are genuine leaders.

"Mark not only leads by example on the field but players respect him for his demeanour off the park. He had a difficult role but he always did well.

"Harry is similar to Mark in terms of passion and desire to succeed. Harry actually got better in his latter years as a Socceroo and the young players coming through idolised him. He was a role model."

* * *

Australia's Ned Zelic, who forged a brilliant career abroad, explained the German football mentality as both countries shaped up for a friendly in Mönchengladbach.

Zelic hails German mentality
24 March 2011

In 1992 Australia's golden boy Ned Zelic, then a promising 21-year-old playmaker who had the world at his feet, got his first taste of Bundesliga football with his new club Borussia Dortmund.

Zelic had just made the giant step of leaving Sydney Olympic for the bright lights of Europe.

He knew only too well that German football would be a tough nut to crack.

What came as a major shock to his system, however, was the intensity behind every tackle, the fierce determination of all the players and their desperate will to win.

"I could not believe it. It was war," Zelic, now 39, said.

What made his baptism of fire most remarkable was the fact that Zelic actually had just taken part in a game at training.

Welcome to German football, Zelic thought, as he recovered from a practice session that was as bruising and competitive as any proper game he had ever played in.

"Training was like a real game and was the biggest shock for me," Zelic said.

"Coming from Australia, I thought it was unbelievable how seriously they took their training. Every minute of every session.

"Players would argue on the field and in the dressing room and go home in a bad mood after a loss at training.

"The competition for places was just incredible. Nothing's changed. They're still the same and that might explain why the Germans are so good at what they do."

Zelic, who is now a television pundit with SBS, is in Germany to take part in a social match involving ex-players of Dortmund, for whom he played until 1995.

Next week he will travel to Mönchengladbach to watch Australia take on Germany in a much-expected friendly match on Wednesday morning (AEDT).

The Socceroos face an enormous task against the Germans who only nine months ago slaughtered them 4-0 in a FIFA World Cup match in Durban.

Germany is arguably the greatest football country in Europe, having won three World Cups, three European Championships and many club tournaments.

As the Socceroos prepare for battle, Zelic was able to give an insight into the German mentality and explain why they are so strong and hard to beat.

Zelic said the overriding impression he got from playing 194 matches for Dortmund, Eintracht Frankfurt and 1860 Munich was the serious way the Germans went about their business.

"They are so efficient and professional about their football and they are seeking perfection all the time," he said.

"Another thing that struck me was how they reacted to wins and losses.

"They never get carried away or paper over any cracks after a victory because there are always things the coach is not happy with so they examine the match thoroughly and try to do even better in the next game.

"Players' heads never drop after a loss either because it is not in their blood. There are no dramas, they just work harder to do better in the next game."

Zelic said German footballers are generally bred on the philosophy that winning is all that matters and if they are going to finish second they might as well finish last.

He also said that the Germans believe that because they usually do not have the natural skills of the Brazilians, Argentines or Spaniards they must compensate with a show of temperament, character and ambition.

"They all set themselves really high goals and they are drilled early on as juniors that winning is everything and second is nothing. All they want is to be number one," Zelic explained.

"They've always been disciplined and athletic and had a team ethic but now they are beginning to focus on the individuals, as the last World Cup showed quite clearly.

"There are other factors that shape the German mentality. For example, Germans are prepared to go through the pain barrier to win a match because they just hate losing.

"Okay, Germans are not the only ones who do this but there are different levels to it and you'll find that the Germans are on the highest level."

Zelic said the mentality of a typical German footballer is best illustrated by his ability to hold his nerve in a penalty shootout.

A shootout is seen as a lottery by most pundits worldwide but try telling that to the German national team, which has hardly ever lost on penalties since they were introduced in the mid-1980s.

"To win a shootout you need mental strength and the Germans have it in abundance," Zelic said.

"That's why they are so much ahead of everyone else in that department."

* * *

Socceroos coach Holger Osieck was under intense pressure after Australia hit plenty of turbulence in their bid to reach the 2014 World Cup. He opened up in a frank chat.

Osieck urges Socceroos to show Aussie grit
16 April 2013

Australia coach Holger Osieck has called on the Socceroos to show a true national spirit as they fight for their lives in the 2014 World Cup campaign.

Australia are engaged in a cut-throat bid to reach the FIFA World Cup and in June they face group leaders Japan in Saitama before entertaining Jordan and Iraq at home.

With only two teams qualifying directly to the finals in Brazil, Osieck's team are sitting third in five-team Group B behind Japan and Jordan.

Osieck said there was no need for fans to panic but he has urged his players to display the grit and temperament that are synonymous with the 'Aussie battler'.

"Australians always lift when they have their backs to the wall and I really hope that the Socceroos players will respond to their qualifying situation with a fighting performance against Japan," Osieck said.

"I have come to realise that the Socceroos are at their best when the going gets tough and this gives me hope because this is also when the tough get going.

"In a way Aussies are like we Germans, who like nothing more than beating the odds."

Osieck spoke at length about the three matches in June that will shape the destiny of Australia's national team.

Were you shocked at how close Australia came to losing at home to Oman?

"I was well prepared for the Oman game and we knew them very well and had a good idea of what to expect. But unfortunately some unpredictable stuff happened. We conceded an early goal and an unlucky own goal early in the second half.

"There also were indications that some players who had never played at that level felt the pressure of the occasion.

"Some players were a bit too tight because everybody wanted us to win and that created a mindset that deprived them from playing to their potential.

"Luckily we bounced back after an intense team talk at halftime and found our rhythm.

"I would not call the 2-2 draw a shock, more like a setback. I would have been shocked if we did not respond, but we did."

You were very agitated during the match. Is this a sign that the pressure is rising?

"Normally I am a bit more composed during a game when it runs according to expectation. But I tried to have an impact on the team from outside and try to lift my team that way.

"I also was annoyed with the time-wasting antics of the Omani team. They were out to disrupt our rhythm from the start with their gamesmanship, which in my book is not right.

"I do not understand that. You always try to gain maximum advantage over your opponent but there is also a code of conduct."

Many fans are deeply concerned about the group situation. Is this because they realise we are not in the comfort zone anymore?

"I don't think we should panic. I said from the very beginning that our qualifying campaign probably might have to go down to our last game versus Iraq.

"We have had a difficult road and the set-up was different to the last campaign because we played many games away in the first half of qualification while Japan had more games at home and got enough points early to be able to cruise while we were forced to trail."

Let's face it, the Socceroos are in a spot of bother. How are they getting out of the hole they have dug themselves in?

"First of all we are still in a position where we can still determine our own fate. If we had been in a situation where we depended on other results to get through, that would be scary.

"So we can still work actively towards qualification. I am convinced we will make it. If I were not convinced I would be the wrong person to lead the team and I would not be here."

Is the Australian team becoming too dependent on Tim Cahill?

"I would not say so. The fact is that when you introduce some new faces you could see that players like Cahill are leading the group in terms of their experience.

"Cahill is in a good mindset at the moment and I am confident he will continue to do a good job for us."

Are you 100 per cent convinced about how best to use Cahill?

"I have no doubt that Cahill, as we saw in the second half against Oman, is best at the top of our attack."

However, Cahill said after the Oman game that he was not getting any joy by playing up front and he had to drop back to create more space for himself.

"But how could he create space for himself when he dropped off and created a vacuum up front? I don't agree with that. We don't need him in midfield. We have enough players in that area and besides, who is going to play up front? I think Cahill is most dangerous when he plays up front."

The A-League will be over soon which will deprive your domestic-based players of competitive games.

"Percentage wise we always have more overseas-based players, anyway. My plan is to pick a dozen or so A-League players and have regular camps in the period of time between the end of the season and the June qualifiers.

"We are working on the logistics of having trial matches against state teams which hopefully will give us the competitive edge."

Some players have shown that they are not quite ready for international football. Did you pick them to appease those who say you have not given new players a chance?

"I never pick players because I have to please anybody. I pick players because I see prospects.

"My job is twofold: one is delivering results that would enable Australia to qualify for Brazil and the other is to develop players.

"I cannot drop some new players after they have a below-par game because as a coach you have to show patience otherwise you lose them. That would not be the right approach."

Are the two demands of your job working against each other?

"It could be the case, yes, so it is crucial that when you use new players you win games. A good example was the friendly match we played against Korea Republic in Hwaseong last year when we had several new faces; we did well and we won 2-1."

Are expectations on the Socceroos too high?

"I'm not too sure what the people are saying because I am ill-informed about what's going on. I am not into the social media and all that stuff."

Do you feel that the media has treated you well so far?

"Again, I do not really know. The media has a job to be critical and report on what it thinks is necessary. You can win a game by a good margin and still get criticised and if you lose it is normal that you receive criticism. It is simply a part of the game."

Japan need a point to qualify and a point would do very nicely for Australia. Can we expect a safety-first match in Saitama?

"Apart from the points situation one aspect of the match will be the rivalry between Japan and Australia.

"Even if it were a friendly it would have been a very tough game. It's all about not giving an inch to the other team and I expect them to have the same attitude. They are a difficult side and I hope that we will be the stronger team on the day."

Australia outplayed Japan before Mark Milligan got sent off in the last qualifier in Brisbane. Does this give you courage for the game in June?

"All you need to do is look back at the Asian Cup final in Doha in 2011. Who were the better team? We lost 1-0 because we made a mistake three minutes from time and we did not finish off a couple of opportunities we had earlier.

"We were stronger in that final and that is what I want us to be in Saitama.

"I want us to play football. Sometimes it is a bit tough because of the opposition's set-up but you should never lose your fire and direction."

Australia have not been playing too well lately. Do you expect a strong reaction in Japan?

"Of course … and it will have to be a team effort. All players who will be on the park that night will have to deliver."

Your contract expires as soon as Australia's involvement in the World Cup comes to an end. Would you be interested in staying on for the 2015 AFC Asian Cup?

"We have not discussed anything. All I can say is that I like it here in Australia. But

I have not even thought about the Asian Cup, to be honest. I've put all my energy into our bid to reach Brazil."

* * *

Coach Holger Osieck was sacked after the Socceroos suffered two humiliating defeats against Brazil and France. But football's problems were more widespread.

Osieck pays the price for our failings
14 October 2013

Sacking Holger Osieck won't solve the many problems facing Australian football.

It's not necessarily just the coach who needed a kick up the backside but the whole football family.

By football family I mean everyone: administrators, clubs, coaches, players, agents, media and fans.

Osieck has paid the price for the Parisian capitulation but if we are honest with ourselves we should be big enough to utter a collective 'mea culpa' for the woes that have beset our game at representative level.

The disgraceful debacles in Brazil and France that yielded a 'dirty dozen' of goals came while the under-20s crashed 5–1 to Vietnam, after the under-17s failed to qualify for their 2013 World Cup and not so long after the Olyroos failed to reach the 2012 London Games and not scoring one goal in the process.

Which suggests that we may have got it wrong at all levels of our game.

So how do we clean up the monumental mess we have got ourselves into?

This is a difficult period in our game's history and it certainly is not the time for finger-pointing because we are all to blame for the current predicament.

Despite several warning signs, the damage has been done and it is imperative that our game gets on its feet again after two devastating blows in the space of five weeks.

Football Federation Australia needs to take its time to pick a national coach because the image and future of the Socceroos are at stake here and it can't afford to get it wrong.

So it is crucially important to establish our top priorities.

Do we appoint a coach just to make us competitive in the FIFA World Cup in Brazil and the AFC Asian Cup in Australia in 2015?

Or do we go for someone who will look at the longer term with no pressure to achieve results in these two major tournaments?

I have a feeling that the incoming coach will be told to make sure Australia gets results in both events, which of course means there is a risk that he will do whatever he thinks is necessary to fulfil his mandate and not worry about the future.

We all know now where this short-sighted approach has taken the game.

The best course of action would appear to be to cut our losses and concentrate on the Asian Cup.

I'm afraid we have metaphorically missed the boat for Brazil but there is still time to assemble a decent team for the Asian Cup.

Yet before we do all that we have to have a good look at the mirror and concede that Australia is still at best a second-rate football nation and we should stop placing excessive expectations on our teams and players.

We should examine if the country's young players are being identified and nurtured in the right way.

We should determine if the time has come for the Socceroos to be led by a domestic coach.

We should make up our mind once and for all about what style of football best suits our culture and character.

Most importantly, we should be big enough to acknowledge our faults and limitations and work our way up with humility.

We also should create an environment where debate and criticism are encouraged rather than dismissed as uncool, agenda driven or even heretical.

This patronising attitude has bred a culture of sychophancy that has given us a false sense of security and delusions of grandeur.

Australia will only become a real football country when it trades its jingoism for realism and its stakeholders replace egoism with altruism for the good of the game.

If the game prospers everybody wins but if it flounders we all lose; let's not forget that.

Sacking coaches is not the answer.

*   *   *

Socceroos defender Lucas Neill marred his reputation as an exemplary leader with his petulant behaviour on and off the field after Australia qualified for the 2014 World Cup.

The own goals that will haunt Neill
25 November 2013

Lucas Neill faces the real prospect of being remembered for all the wrong reasons as his extraordinary international career draws closer to an end.

Neill, 35, has played 96 times for Australia, 61 of them as captain.

He has been a loyal servant to his country for many years but the scrutiny he has faced in the last two years or so has brought out a side in him that we had never seen.

Neill is under siege as new coach Ange Postecoglou embarks on a rejuvenation of the Socceroos squad with the 2014 FIFA World Cup in Brazil only seven months away.

His position in the team is under serious threat and his frustration or perhaps even his insecurity came to the fore last week when he reacted poorly to a series of boos directed at him by spectators during the international win over Costa Rica.

Neill's abuse at the fans during play was unbecoming of such an experienced player and Football Federation Australia chief executive David Gallop was forced to publicly berate his behaviour as "unacceptable".

Being a perfectly normal human being, it would appear that Neill was right to tell his abusers to go jump in the river when he and the team were doing nothing wrong.

Neill, however, tends to forget that as captain he should be more careful about what he does or says and how he is seen to be doing or saying things.

His unflattering appraisal of the younger generation's contribution to the national team in the wake of the two heavy defeats to Brazil and France in the space of a month also raised a few eyebrows.

It was not the kind of talk any young player dreaming of an international breakthrough would have liked to hear from the captain, who seemed to be partly blaming their "lack of hunger" for the two debacles.

Neill later explained—not entirely convincingly—that his comments were designed to bring the best out of the young aspirants.

Yet he should have done it privately, not publicly.

These instances were not the only times that football fans were led to shake their heads by Neill's attitude.

In one of his first matches as Socceroos captain under then coach Pim Verbeek, Neill was talking about the 2010 World Cup qualifier against China in Kunming.

Neill could have caused a few awkward moments for the Australians after he declared that playing in China comes with its special difficulties, such as dodgy food and hotels and team buses not making it in time for training and so forth.

Any Australian who has played in parts of Asia would probably relate to and agree with Neill's sentiments but, again, the point is that as skipper sometimes he should refrain from telling it the way it is because you never know how such comments can be taken.

Neill, not unlike Harry Kewell, comes across as a very private and somewhat aloof person.

He also believes that he is being victimised by fans and media.

There is no doubt that he is under severe pressure to retain his place in the team, possibly even from FFA, which has noticeably failed to back him when he most needed support.

And surely he must justifiably feel that some of the vitriol directed at him is disrespectful of his position and unappreciative of what he's done for the team over the years.

He repaid the faith shown in him by Postecoglou by putting in a decent performance against the Costa Ricans, although it must be said that the Ticos were as soft as expected and hardly ever troubled Mat Ryan in goal.

Neill is his own man and has been around long enough not to need too much advice from his people anymore.

But if he wants to be remembered as one of Australia's finest and most accomplished defenders of all time he must have a good look in the mirror and change his ways that have not endeared him to the public.

He certainly is not the reliable defender he used to be and whom we all admired but he is still a pretty decent footballer who is strong enough to play in Brazil, essentially because there appears to be no one good and experienced enough to replace him.

He now has seven months to repair his tainted image.

The ball is in his court.

*   *   *

Manfred Schaefer had given up hope of ever getting the Socceroos cap he richly deserved ... but 47 years after making his international debut he was surprised at a '1974' get-together.

Socceroos legend Schaefer finally gets his cap

15 June 2014

It has taken 47 years but Australia legend Manfred Schaefer has finally got his Socceroos cap.

The robust defender was presented with the cherished cap during a function marking the 40th anniversary of the Socceroos' first ever match in the FIFA World Cup.

Schaefer, who played for Australia against East Germany on 14 June 1974, made his debut for the Socceroos against New Zealand in Saigon (now Ho Chi Minh City) in November 1967 and went on to play 49 international matches.

However, he only got his cap during the function hosted by Marconi Club at the weekend.

"They've been trying for four or five years to give me the cap," Schaefer, who is now 71, said.

"But I am not the type to go up in front of a big crowd before an international game to get my cap.

"My daughter has been upset with me for not going to get it because she said I deserve it. So I thought the chance might have passed me by.

"I knew something was going on at the function because when the subject of the cap came up everybody changed the subject.

"But now when I look at it and see I'm the 198th player to represent my country I remember the day I made my debut in a tournament in Saigon.

"I was not picked to play against New Zealand but coach Joe Vlasits put me on just before halftime after Frank Micic got injured.

"And once I got into the team there was no way I was going to lose my place unless I was not good enough."

Schaefer said he has grown somewhat disillusioned with the football hierarchy's failure to duly acknowledge the feats of his fellow semi-professionals who put Australia on the world map by qualifying for the 16-team 1974 World Cup.

"The idea that football in Australia started only in 2006 is a kick in the guts as far as I'm concerned and if I never got my cap it would not have worried me at all," he said.

"You cannot delete history. We were the first Socceroos to put Australia on the map. Nobody can take that away from us."

Schaefer is still regarded as one of Australia's toughest and most reliable defenders.

He played his last match for Australia in the third 1974 World Cup group match against Chile in Berlin that ended in a 0-0 draw.

* * *

In the build-up to the 2015 AFC Asian Cup on home soil, the Socceroos were showing signs that Ange Postecoglou's work would be rewarded.

Socceroos deserve some tender loving care

8 September 2014

The new-look Australia team that are still reeling from three defeats at the 2014 FIFA World Cup need all the support they can get as they shape up for the 2015 AFC Asian Cup on home soil.

'QUOTE UNQUOTE'

After suffering their sixth defeat in eight matches since coach Ange Postecoglou took over less than a year ago, fans would be entitled to feel nervous about their favourite team.

Coaches usually get sacked for that sort of record.

After a comprehensive 2-0 defeat to Belgium in the international in Liege, the general concern about the current Socceroos must have grown a notch or two.

The boys were outplayed by a slick Belgian side that were not at full strength but the Socceroos showed in patches what they can achieve if they reduce their alarming mistake rate.

Okay, you don't play matches in patches, particularly at the highest level.

Yet the intrepid Socceroos unquestionably have shown promising signs in their last four matches in Brazil and Belgium to suggest that the good times might not be too far off.

Which means that we should be patient and tolerant in our treatment of this side because, despite the doom and gloom emanating from the scoreboard, it can so easily flourish right in time for the Asian Cup in January.

Patience is not a word you would usually associate with Australia's football culture.

For far too long Aussie footballers have tried to get to the opposing goal and win matches as quickly as possible while the fans and media have always demanded almost instant success.

However, as Postecoglou tries to change the team's mentality in favour of a more measured approach, the fans should temper their expectations.

We all knew that Postecoglou's revolution that ushered in generation next was going to be painful before being gainful.

We all recognised that the task of replacing the veteran heroes who put Australia on the world map was never going to be a walk in the park.

And we all accepted the inescapable fact that the new players coming in would need time to fit into Postecoglou's modern methods and adapt to the unforgiving demands of international football.

Results so far might suggest that things are not going according to plan but let's not forget that there already have been some success stories.

The new team have shown that they can take on some of the world's best and give a good account of themselves if only in fleeting moments of a game.

Speedy striker Mathew Leckie does not seem at all out of place on the right side of the attack and he would be a far more devastating player if he sharpens his distribution.

Exciting if inconsistent winger Tommy Oar has acquitted himself well on the other side of the attack and, again, he would be more influential with better crossing.

There is not much more one can say about Mark Bresciano, who continues to boost his legendary status in our game by showing guile, smartness and vision in midfield at 34 years of age.

He will be terribly missed when he eventually pulls the plug on his incredible career.

Uncompromising midfielder Mark Milligan, whose international career was in limbo a few years ago, has fitted in beautifully in Postecoglou's system and it was his opening to Jason Davidson in the first half that provided Bresciano with one of Australia's two best scoring chances against the Belgians.

Young Mat Ryan had big shoes to fill when he took over from the incomparable Mark Schwarzer but he already has established himself as the number one goalkeeper.

Australia are lucky to be able to count on his agility, alertness and positional sense for years to come.

Postecoglou's main problems lie in the back four.

There is still a worrying level of misunderstanding and a glaring lack of pace in the back third that will need to be fixed if the Socceroos are to make a serious bid to win the Asian Cup.

Aggressive captain Mile Jedinak does his darndest to protect his erratic defenders in his screening role but he can only do so much.

Belgium got behind Australia's defence far too many times and the first goal they scored was a result of a collective comedy of errors that would have deeply annoyed Postecoglou.

Australia just cannot afford to keep making such schoolboy mistakes in the Asian Cup because the quick forwards from Japan and Korea Republic could rip through their defence with ease.

Having said that, it is therefore vital for the media and fans to be patient and tolerant in their treatment of a team that are prepared to take a few risks and have a go.

This is what we all wanted to see after the bleak years of Pim Verbeek and Holger Osieck, after all.

In Postecoglou the Socceroos have a competent coach and supreme motivator who has a vision and knows what he's doing.

His selected players need to know that they will not be vilified or punished as soon as they have a poor game.

Today's elite Socceroos are not the finest players in the world—many would argue they are not even among Australia's best ever—but they are showing enough enterprise and bravery as a team and individually to deserve to be persevered with.

I have a feeling that if we are patient enough with this lot the rewards will come for one and all.

* * *

'QUOTE UNQUOTE'

World Cup defender Alex Wilkinson realised his dream of winning a league title after years of frustration and heartbreak ... but he had to join Jeonbuk in Korea to do so.

Wilkinson finally savours a league title
9 November 2014

Australia defender Alex Wilkinson conceded he had feared he would never win a championship as a professional footballer after he celebrated the first league title in his career.

Wilkinson, 30, realised his elusive dream at the weekend when he helped Jeonbuk Motors clinch the K League Classic title.

An away 3-0 win over Jeju United gave Jeonbuk the championship with three matches to spare.

Wilkinson played in three losing A-League grand finals with Central Coast Mariners in 2006, 2008 and 2011 and finished second in the K League with Jeonbuk in 2012.

But on Saturday night, five months after playing for Australia at the FIFA World Cup in Brazil, he finally tasted sweet success after years of bitter memories.

"I really thought I'd never win a league championship," Wilkinson said.

"I was definitely due a championship, that's for sure, after coming so close so many times.

"We have had a great season at Jeonbuk and we thoroughly deserved the championship, winning it with three games to spare, so it's a great feeling.

"I came so close with the Mariners obviously, losing three grand finals.

"I guess when I came to Jeonbuk I was hopeful of winning a league title as they are a pretty big club in Korea.

"My first year here we finished second and last year we came third while losing the FA Cup final on penalties. So this year it's great to finally get some silverware."

Wilkinson has one more season left in his contract with Jeonbuk and he is looking forward to the club's participation in the AFC Champions League in 2015.

"Yes, I think the Champions League is our next target now," he explained.

"Jeonbuk lost the final on penalties in 2011 so they have come close before. Our coach places a big emphasis on the Champions League and we were disappointed to be eliminated this year in the second round.

"We will lose a few good players to the army next year so hopefully we can find replacements and I think with the squad we have we can have a good ACL campaign."

Wilkinson flies out to Japan on Monday to link up with Ange Postecoglou's Socceroos squad as it prepares for the international match against Japan in Osaka on 18 November.

"Korea to Japan is only a two-hour flight which is nice for a change," he said.

"I'm looking forward to this camp. Japan and Australia have had a great rivalry since our move into Asia.

"Playing them in their own backyard will be a good test of where we are at.

"They are a strong team with some very good individuals so it's another challenge we are looking forward to."

Wilkinson said the football community in the Korea Republic is still coming to terms with the national team's disappointing World Cup campaign in Brazil.

Australia and Korea Republic are in the same group in the Asian Cup and they meet on match day three in Brisbane.

"I think they are under some pressure to have a decent tournament in Australia," Wilkinson said.

"They have a new coach (Uli Stielike) since the World Cup as the whole country was very angry and disappointed about the way they performed in Brazil.

"It will be a big game up in Brisbane, for sure. A few of my teammates from Jeonbuk have a good chance of being selected in the Korean squad which is good for the club."

* * *

Australian football snared the first major honour in its long history when Ange Postecoglou's Socceroos won the 2015 Asian Cup amid widespread acclaim.

Triumphant Socceroos take the game to next level
1 February 2015

The Socceroos ushered in a new era for the game in Australia by snaring the first major honour in their long and colourful history.

A goal in extra time from substitute James Troisi gave the Socceroos a 2-1 victory over Korea Republic.

A sublime strike from rising star and player of the tournament Massimo Luongo had given Ange Postecoglou's men the lead on a night of raw passion at Stadium Australia.

But when it looked like the Socceroos had done enough to win the match, up popped star player Son Heung-min with an injury-time goal to send the contest into extra time.

Troisi snatched the winning goal when he stabbed the ball home from close range.

It was nothing less than the Australians deserved and they now can look forward to a period of sustained growth with the belief that in master coach Postecoglou they have a leader who will continue to make the team the swashbuckling and adventurous outfit we all want to see.

"The goal in the last minute really tested us as a group," a relieved Postecoglou said later.

"But the players stood up once again and full credit to them. I couldn't be more proud of them and it's great for our country.

"Credit to Korea, I thought the two best sides were in the grand final, playing off for the trophy.

"It was a game worthy of bringing the champion out and I thought the boys showed those championship qualities tonight."

It was not always pretty but, as they say, when the going gets tough, the tough get going.

The Socceroos showed what they are made of in winning the trophy, turning it on when they needed to and fighting to the death when the occasion warranted it, as was the case in the final.

And the crowd responded brilliantly, riding every tackle, cheering every clearance, jeering every Korean mistake and raising the roof of the place when Australia scored.

Stadium Australia is only 16 years old but it already holds a special place in the hearts of Socceroos fans.

The national team do not have a national stadium where they play their big matches like England do.

Yet the maligned arena that was the centrepiece of the 2000 Olympics has become the spiritual home of the Socceroos.

Many feel the stands are too far from the action and if not full the stadium lacks atmosphere.

Yet when the 80,000 stadium is almost bursting at the seams as it was for this compelling final it becomes a coliseum of passion, colour and sound.

It was here that John Aloisi scored the famous penalty against Uruguay that took the green and gold to the 2006 FIFA World Cup.

And it was here that Josh Kennedy popped up with the match-winning header that gave the Socceroos their ticket to the 2014 World Cup.

Both teams went into the final match with guns blazing and in search of a rare moment of glory on the international front.

The Socceroos had a first major honour in their sights while the Taeguk Warriors sought their first Asian title since 1960.

A physical and uncompromising confrontation between two old rivals was always on the cards and that is how it panned out.

Korea had their chances in the first half, emanating mostly from the cultured feet of Son who was a constant menace to Australia's defence with his positive runs on and off the ball.

At one stage only a desperate, lunging tackle from Luongo prevented the Bayer Leverkusen striker from opening the scoring.

Luongo's contribution to the Socceroos' cause took a dramatic turn just before halftime when he produced an example of his prodigious talents with a memorable goal.

He received a deep pass from Trent Sainsbury, took a touch with his right foot, then another with his left and from the edge of the penalty area beat Kim Jin-su with a low shot to the corner of the net.

The same net that meant so much to Aloisi and Kennedy over the years.

It was the first goal Korea had conceded in the whole tournament.

"We set out on this journey before the World Cup and I think the boss put the main thing forward that we have to have belief in ourselves because the boys we have and the type of group we have is different than most clubs and national teams," Luongo said.

"He said together we can make history and we have. No words can describe it."

The Socceroos would not let Son's dramatic equaliser dampen their spirit or soften their resolve to win the trophy and just before the end of the first period of extra time Troisi wrote himself into the history books with his opportunistic goal.

At the Aloisi end of the ground, of course.

* * *

An explosive book by Ange Postecoglou revealed how the former Socceroos coach sacked fallen idol Lucas Neill from the 2014 World Cup squad.

Postecoglou tells of the phone call to sack Neill
24 October 2016

Australia's Ange Postecoglou has revealed that one of the few low points of his coaching career was the day he had to tell Socceroos hero Lucas Neill he was not going to the 2014 FIFA World Cup ... on the phone.

Postecoglou took a rejuvenated squad to the tournament in Brazil that had no room for Neill, who captained the Socceroos in the 2010 World Cup in South Africa.

Postecoglou, who had taken over the job of national coach in October 2013, has told of how he had to inform Neill that his international career was over, four matches short of a 100 caps.

"I didn't have any problems with the guys who'd made their own call (to retire). I did struggle with the Lucas Neill situation though," Postecoglou writes in his book *Changing the Game*.

"Being the captain and leader of the country for such a long time, Lucas had had a celebrated career. Regrettably it finished at the end of a phone call.

"The end for Lucas shouldn't have been a call from me telling him he wasn't going to the 2014 World Cup.

"Denial about career ending is a huge thing for many players. Delivering that final message is perhaps the most unpleasant part of my job.

"I do wonder if, with Lucas Neill, there was another way."

Postecoglou wanted to fly to London to give Neill the bad news in person but, with preparations for the World Cup gathering momentum, he simply ran out of time.

"I just had to make that phone call. It still rankles," Postecoglou says.

"As phone calls go, it was a strange one. The pleasantries didn't take long to complete and Lucas began presenting his case.

"He'd played in an under-21s game and was getting stronger. He was trying to convince himself as much as me, I think.

"He said he'd had an issue with his hamstring but that was done with now and his progress had been very good.

"I had to interject. 'Lucas, it's gone too far. I've got to make the call now. Because of who you are I think it's better I make the call early, rather than have to drag on and muddy the waters later on. Let's deal with it now. You're not coming to Brazil'.

"The phone went quiet before I heard 'Okay'. I told him it was his news to handle how he wanted. He made it clear he would not be saying anything. 'I'll go to ground. If you change your mind let me know because I'm playing in a game next week'.

"I wasn't going to change my mind. It's almost three years since that phone call and he hasn't surfaced so he was true to his word.

"He seems to have gone into hiding and I sort of wish that wasn't so for one of our greatest-ever Socceroos."

Australia went on to meet Chile (1–3), the Netherlands (2–3) and Spain (0–3) in Brazil before they won the 2015 AFC Asian Cup in Australia in January.

* * *

Ange Postecoglou's decision to go with three at the back backfired as the Socceroos continued to struggle in their campaign to reach the 2018 World Cup.

Postecoglou's tactical gamble backfires
24 March 2017

Australia's stuttering campaign to reach the 2018 FIFA World Cup is slipping out of their hands and is now in the lap of the gods.

After yet another hugely disappointing performance against Iraq in neutral Tehran, the Socceroos should thank their lucky stars for emerging with a point from a 1–1 draw that left their World Cup campaign hanging by a thread.

As things stand with four rounds to go, Saudi Arabia and Japan lead Group B with 13 points each. Australia are third with 10, one ahead of United Arab Emirates.

Two teams go through automatically while the third best team will have to successfully negotiate two home-and-away playoffs to reach the finals.

The big event in Russia seemed a million miles away as Ange Postecoglou's disjointed team struggled to overcome feisty opponents on a terrible pitch and in a brand-new formation.

For the first time the coach went with only three at the back in a move designed to reduce the risk of his team being caught out when it loses possession, particularly high up the field.

He hoped that three defenders would give him a better balance and the insurance of an extra man when the opposition counter-attack because the Socceroos have been caught napping a few times in recent matches due to the fact that both fullbacks were too far up, leaving the two central defenders exposed.

Well, the pattern did not work in Tehran because the Iraqis went through Australia's five-man midfield almost at will for most of the match despite Aaron Mooy's industry in the middle of the park.

The Iraqis could have had three goals before the Socceroos opened the scoring just before halftime with a header from Mathew Leckie.

Iraq's equaliser came as no surprise and how the Australians survived a barrage from the 'home' side that desperately needed a win to stay in the race for Russia will remain a mystery.

Australia's midfield collapsed in the second half and it is a sign of how poorly the team performed that goalkeeper Mitch Langerak stole the show with two jaw-dropping saves that he had no right to make.

Postecoglou ought to be commended for trying things in his efforts to find the right formula that would take his team to the World Cup.

He is a staunch believer in 4-3-3 which earned the Socceroos the 2015 AFC Asian Cup but he has dabbled with 4-4-2 and now a sort of 3-2-3-2 but the sad fact remains that Postecoglou, despite his positivity, is limited in the quality personnel required for the team to make a mark on the world game.

He was dead right when he said the team has gone backwards since it won the Asian Cup just over two years ago.

Very few of his men are playing regularly at an acceptable standard and those who are are not delivering for their country.

The Socceroos are no well-oiled machine at the moment.

This glaring weakness showed in consecutive lacklustre displays against Saudi Arabia, Japan, Thailand and Iraq. All matches finished in uninspiring draws but the Socceroos could so easily have lost them all.

It remains to be seen if Postecoglou will persist with the 'three at the back' formation against the UAE in Sydney on Tuesday and give it another chance to flourish.

It is the first of three must-win home games for the Socceroos in the next few months.

The Socceroos will have no excuses if they fail to beat the UAE, who lost 2-0 to Japan in Al Ain a few hours after the stalemate in Tehran.

Postecoglou and his men have an opportunity to get things right in familiar surroundings, get their campaign back on track with a strong performance and hope that other results go their way.

Let's get this straight. The situation for the Socceroos is not precarious and there is enough time left for recovery.

But one thing is beyond any doubt: if they keep playing like this and do not lift their game considerably they will not make the World Cup.

* * *

Socceroos coach Ange Postecoglou shocked the football family midstream by declaring he would quit his position at the end of the 2018 World Cup qualifying campaign.

Socceroos the big losers in Postecoglou quit saga
12 October 2017

The Socceroos players themselves are the biggest losers in the dramatic events surrounding national coach Ange Postecoglou's pending departure that have all the makings of a soap opera.

Postecoglou will desert the very players he has worked with for three years after next month's 2018 FIFA World Cup playoff against Honduras.

Less than a day after he led his side to a battling 3-2 aggregate victory over modest Syria, it emerged that Postecoglou will relinquish his post regardless of the outcome of the clash with the Central Americans.

Postecoglou has had an opportunity to deny the reports revealing his intentions to quit but he did not do so.

The reasons for Postecoglou's shock decision are unknown.

It has been suggested that his relationship with Football Federation Australia is tense and terse.

It has also been claimed that he is not prepared to take the strong criticism that the Socceroos' timid performances in the last few months have warranted.

It is also believed he might have a club job lined up abroad.

Whatever the reason for his faux pas, Postecoglou has done the wrong thing by the players who see him as the man to help them realise their World Cup dream.

As things stand now, they would be perfectly entitled to feel disappointed at best and badly let down at worst.

Can you imagine the players' frame of mind when they go into the forthcoming tie with the Hondurans, knowing that their coach will not be there to guide them at the World Cup should they prevail?

Can Postecoglou look at his players with a straight face and urge them to give everything for the green and gold jersey when he himself will abandon them at the final whistle?

And can Postecoglou expect his players who must feel they are in limbo to keep sticking to a system of play that some of them do not even understand—if rumours about unease are to be believed—when they know it could all change after he goes?

This is not the first time Postecoglou has jumped ship. After he led Brisbane Roar to two A-League championships in 2011 and 2012 he was expected to keep his promise to hang around for an attempt at a treble.

What did he do next? He quit Brisbane to join Melbourne Victory, leaving several Roar players dumbfounded and feeling let down.

The same must apply to the current Socceroos' squad members, which is really a sorry state of affairs.

I have supported Postecoglou ever since he took on the Brisbane job and went about transforming the way we play our football.

The Socceroos also gained significantly from Postecoglou's expertise and captured the hearts of a nation by winning the AFC Asian Cup in early 2015.

But Postecoglou appears to have lost the plot in recent months and some of his statements and decisions raised many eyebrows.

His inflated opinion of the A-League and Australian footballers was clearly designed to instil confidence and ultimately remove our innate inferiority complex but these things tend to come back to bite you if things get a bit sticky.

And his obsession with turning the Socceroos into a team playing 'his' style of football simply has not worked, particularly when he changed the team's formation midway through the qualifying campaign.

Good national coaches do not ram philosophies down their players' throats but see what is available and play the game accordingly.

Club coaches buy players they need to fit their plans but national coaches have to make do with what is available.

This is something Postecoglou seems to have failed to understand.

Postecoglou has done a lot for Australian football but in his manic drive to improve our playing standard and mentality he forgot that doing it his way was not always possible.

"I have not lost faith in what I do," he told Fairfax a few days ago.

The trouble is many people have lost faith in what Postecoglou is doing.

* * *

Three months before Australia faced Denmark in the 2018 World Cup, Danish captain Simon Kjaer revealed his team's frame of mind in an exclusive interview.

Denmark captain Kjaer fears Aussies' experience
31 March 2018

Denmark captain Simon Kjaer admitted that Australia will have a distinct advantage when the two teams clash in a group match at the 2018 FIFA World Cup in Russia.

The Danes and Socceroos are in Group C along with France and Peru and will meet in Samara on June 22 (AEST).

Kjaer, who plays his club football for Spain's Sevilla and will face Bayern Munich in the UEFA Champions League quarter-finals next week, said Bert van Marwijk's men are more seasoned campaigners in international tournaments.

"Some people in Denmark have claimed that this is not a difficult group for us—maybe rather the opposite—but I do not agree," Kjaer, 29, said.

"Australia are a strong team with valuable experience from major tournaments such as the World Cup, Asian Cup and Confederations Cup.

"This is something we lack in Denmark after having not qualified for the last six years for the World Cup or the Euros.

"Australia are Asian champions and that says a lot about their quality. Their latest results could confuse a bit but they don't really confuse me because in trial matches you never really know.

"A draw with Colombia is a top-class result whereas losing to Norway is obviously less impressive."

Denmark and Australia qualified for the World Cup finals via a playoff.

The Danes overcame Ireland 5-1 in Dublin after a home 0-0 draw thanks largely to a hat-trick from Tottenham Hotspur hotshot Christian Eriksen while the Socceroos had a treble from Aston Villa's Mile Jedinak to thank for a 3-1 win over Honduras after a 0-0 draw in San Pedro Sula.

Kjaer, who plays in the centre of defence, said there is little difference between the two teams even though Denmark (12) are ranked much higher than Australia (37).

He acknowledges that the flamboyant French are the team to beat in the group.

"When you look at the world rankings we are three teams in the top 12 right now and that shows real high quality," he said.

"But the FIFA rankings do not give the full picture ... they also tell us that France, Peru and ourselves win a lot of matches which is why we occupy such high positions.

"Obviously France look like the favourites to win our group. If the French live up to their potential, they are definitely among the top contenders for the world championship ... and you cannot really say that about the rest of us.

"I believe that we look very even in level but let's see. It's a very competitive group and we are looking forward to that challenge. It is our clear goal to advance from the group stage but I am pretty sure that we share that goal with Australia and Peru."

Kjaer admitted he does not know much about the Australian team but he knows that the Socceroos do not have a reputation as great competitors for nothing.

"They are a hardworking, well-organised and honest football team," he said.

"As I said, Australia have a lot of World Cup experience since this is their fourth straight finals appearance. They also have experience from other tournaments like the Asian Cup and Confederations Cup and they will surely benefit from that in Russia.

"I know Maty Ryan privately. We have met because we have the same agent and he is a great guy. As a football player I know him to be super professional and a great goalie, which he proves now in the Premier League."

Kjaer, who missed the first part of the year due to a calf injury, is back in full swing and he played a key role in Sevilla's defeat of Manchester United in the UCL's round of 16.

He was back in the Danish team that played two internationals in the most recent FIFA break.

They beat Panama 1–0 in Brondby and drew 0–0 with Chile in Aalborg.

So what are Denmark's strengths?

"As Denmark captain I am happy to say that the team spirit is our greatest strength," he said.

"We laugh together but we also bleed together and we will work hard to do anything to help each other. Every single member of this group of players knows and appreciates that we are nothing without each other.

"That is not necessarily the truth about all teams in football. But we share that feeling and ability and that makes the unit stronger than just 11 individuals in the same jerseys.

"I enjoyed having Morten Olsen as national coach but then he left us two years ago and Aage Hareide took over with a new style and new ideas. It has changed our way of playing—we got more flexibility in our systems, we can change our game plan and that made us more difficult to read."

* * *

Graham Arnold admitted after taking over from Bert van Marwijk as national coach that he was not ready for the Socceroos job in 2007.

Arnold reveals Asian Cup rift with Neill, Aloisi
9 August 2018

Incoming Socceroos coach Graham Arnold admitted he did not deserve the national job in 2007 that put him offside with FIFA World Cup stalwarts Lucas Neill and John Aloisi and urged fans not to judge him on the ill-fated AFC Asian Cup campaign.

Arnold was in charge of the Socceroos side that stuttered to the quarter-finals of the Asian Cup. It was a position he admits he did not deserve.

Arnold's appointment as Socceroos coach for the next four years was not met with universal approval and the 55-year-old vowed to do his utmost to win over the sceptics.

"I'm here to do my best and I respect all the fans," Arnold said after his first press conference as national coach.

"The Asian Cup was a long time ago and I have learned from my mistakes so fans should not judge me on 2007.

"I did not deserve to be coach back then … it was a job I inherited and which I did not really want. I was Olympic coach at the time and I helped the organisation out until a new coach was found to replace Guus Hiddink.

"I can tell you that Neill, Aloisi and those guys did not respect me at the time.

"But they do now because they know I've travelled the world and learned a lot of lessons. People in all walks of life make mistakes but that was 11 years ago and I have improved as a coach and a person.

"And regarding the fans (who might have been sceptical about my appointment), it is my job to change their minds and make sure they're happy. I do not have any fear of that.

"I mixed with a lot of fans in Russia during the World Cup which was something I enjoyed very much. They probably saw a different side of me."

The concern among those that opposed Arnold's appointment may stem from the fact that Arnold is seen as a pragmatic coach who will make sure his teams do not lose a match before they try to win it.

Arnold, who has won two A-League championships with Central Coast Mariners and Sydney FC, defended his tactical mentality vehemently, saying he's "a cross between (defensive) Bert van Marwijk and (attacking) Ange Postecoglou".

"I'm a winner. I have principles and they are all designed to win," he explained.

"Statistics around the world show that the winning teams are those with the best defensive records.

"If you look at the A-League records you will see that the Mariners and Sky Blues had the best defensive record when they won the title.

"It's a cliché but the best form of defence is attack but it is also true that you will need to know how to defend when you have an off day."

* * *

The Sydney Football Stadium, that closed its doors for good in late 2019 before it was demolished, was the scene of some of Australian football's most memorable moments.

Stadium curtain falls but Maradona magic lives on
29 September 2018

Allianz Stadium in Sydney has been the stage for some of Australian football's finest moments since it opened its doors to the public in 1988.

Millions of football fans have converged on the arena that is affectionately known by its original name, the Sydney Football Stadium.

It has hosted FIFA World Cup qualifiers, A-League grand finals, Sydney derbies and even a World Youth Cup final.

It also was the stage for some virtuoso individual performances.

Who can ever forget the rocket Charlie Yankos unleashed against Argentina in the 1988 Gold Cup?

Or Mark Schwarzer's shootout heroics against Canada in a World Cup playoff in 1993?

Or Mark Bresciano's spectacular volley against Bahrain in an Asian Cup qualifier in 2006?

Or Alessandro Del Piero's four beauties for Sydney FC against Wellington Phoenix in 2013?

Big stars like Romario, Jose Luis Chilavert, Franco Baresi, Gary Lineker, Diego Maradona, Gabriel Batistuta, Jean-Pierre Papin, Dwight Yorke, Juninho, Shinji Ono and Hakan Sukur also thrilled the more discerning fans at Moore Park with their special skills.

The good ol' SFS has had its critics but nevertheless a degree of loss and sadness will accompany the moment when it closes its doors for good after crooner Michael Bublé gives a one-off concert on Friday night.

Work on the ground's demolition and subsequent redevelopment will commence in January.

The ground has seen several memorable matches over the years but the biggest moment in its history no doubt came on a balmy evening on November 17 in 1993 when Australia faced Argentina in the first leg of a playoff for the final spot at the 1994 World Cup in the United States.

It was a match that ticked all the boxes. It captivated the world's attention and drew a massive global television audience.

Firstly, because two-time world champions Argentina were in serious trouble after crashing to a humiliating 5–0 loss to Colombia in Buenos Aires that forced them into a do-or-die decider with Eddie Thomson's Socceroos.

Secondly, because the tie signalled superstar Maradona's return to the game after a 15-month suspension for cocaine use.

The eagerly awaited tie that captured the imagination of Australia's media was engulfed in controversy before it even kicked off.

Australia's decision to play the first match at home drew strong criticism in the media because it is generally considered that playing a return game at home carries a slight advantage.

Cash-strapped Australian Soccer Federation were accused of opting to play at home first so as to guarantee a full house and eliminate the risk of a blowout score in an away first leg that could have reduced the return to a 'dead rubber'.

But the late Thomson was adamant that his intrepid Socceroos' best chance of surprising their celebrated opponents with a win was by playing first on familiar territory. He had his way.

Thomson's view is corroborated by Paul Wade, Australia's captain on the day.

"That was exactly Eddie's approach all along," Wade says.

"He was banking on a positive result to take to Buenos Aires. Can you imagine the immense pressure the Argentines would have been under if they had to overturn a defeat? Mind you, we still scared the living daylights out of them."

It is all part of our history now how the Socceroos and Albiceleste played out a thrilling 1-1 draw at a 'football friendly' stadium that was bursting at the seams.

Maradona, who told me at the team hotel in Coogee a few days before the match that quality attackers were not given adequate protection by referees, won the ball from Milan Ivanovic on the right and made enough space for himself with some deft footwork to lay on a cross for striker Abel Balbo to beat Mark Bosnich with a sumptuous header to the near post.

Australia replied with a slick team goal just before halftime.

Playmaker Ned Zelic floated a pass into space for overlapping fullback Tony Vidmar who promptly volleyed low for his brother Aurelio to get in front of two defenders and slot home past the outstretched legs of goalkeeper Sergio Goycoechea.

The return at the historic Monumental was always going to be difficult for the Australians and it was made even harder when just before the hour mark striker Gabriel Batistuta hit a speculative ball from an impossible angle that bounced off Alex Tobin's shin and arched its way into the net past the helpless Robert Zabica.

Australia battled bravely and were eventually beaten by a better and more experienced side ... but who knows what could have happened had they taken a couple of half chances that fell their way late in the game?

Maradona went on to play in his fourth World Cup but his image was irrevocably tarnished when he sensationally tested positive to ephedrine after a match with Nigeria and was kicked out of the competition in America. He would never play again for his country.

Australian fans were just grateful that Maradona had played his part in a momentous Sydney occasion that, albeit briefly, put our football on the world map.

It was an event that was etched in the chequered 30-year history of the Sydney Football Stadium.

* * *

'QUOTE UNQUOTE'

The Socceroos opened their 2019 AFC Asian Cup campaign with a shock 1-0 loss to Jordan and Tom Rogic's poor display caused serious concern.

Is Rogic a luxury the Socceroos can ill afford?
7 January 2019

The time has come to pose the question we thought we would never ask. Is Socceroos midfielder Tom Rogic an asset or a liability?

The Celtic star, whose call-up for the 2019 AFC Asian Cup caused plenty of angst in the green half of Glasgow, went missing and was conspicuous by his 'absence' in Australia's opening 1-0 defeat to Jordan in Group B in Al Ain.

The Socceroos played one of their worst and most frustrating matches in months and the gritty Jordanians were full value for an unexpected victory that puts Graham Arnold's men under pressure to reach the last 16 phase.

Rogic was seen as the man who could make the difference to an injury-hit side due to his special qualities that have wooed the faithful at Parkhead.

But Al Ain would be a paradise lost for Rogic.

The Socceroos struggled to break down the well-organised opposition and needed somebody to lead by example but for all he produced in an eminently forgettable afternoon Rogic could well have stayed in Glasgow.

He looked lethargic, he lacked ideas when on the ball, his passing was often erratic and his shooting was way off the mark.

He even managed to sky a ball with his left foot when it looked like it was easier to score than miss from four metres out.

Arnold is one of Rogic's biggest fans but the time has come for the coach to bite the bullet and examine whether Rogic is all that he is cracked up to be in terms of his contribution to the green and gold jersey and whether someone like Jackson Irvine, who is less gifted but physically and temperamentally superior, would be a better alternative as a starter.

Rogic no doubt has the skills and he can be an absolute joy to watch when in full flight with the ball at his feet but he produces the numbers of high class too infrequently to be of constant value to the team.

This is not the first time Rogic played poorly for Australia but we always tend to be mesmerised by his strengths and dismiss his weaknesses as aberrations. But it now might be a case of enough is enough.

It is probably rather churlish to make Rogic the scapegoat for a bad defeat, especially when you remember that playing with inferior players to the ones he is used to playing with in Scotland does not help his game.

But as one of the most experienced players in the squad it is not unreasonable for fans to expect something special from him and feel let down when he does not provide it, let alone perform abysmally as he did against Jordan.

The whole team were terrible as a unit even though they had lots of ball in the second half.

However, possession means nothing if you do not do much with it.

The Socceroos created a few semi-decent scoring chances mainly through young striker Awer Mabil but Jordan were probably just as dangerous in their fewer attacks.

Arnold's attempt to have an interchangeable attack comprising three forwards did not work because the team lacked width and when Australia did widen their attack with a few meaningful forays from fullbacks Aziz Behich and substitute Rhyan Grant, the team looked slightly better without actually being all that dangerous.

Essentially because Arnold has not solved the major problem he inherited since taking up the position after the 2018 FIFA World Cup: an inability to stick the ball in the net.

The Socceroos are like toothless tigers.

Scoring goals is still Australia's Achilles heel, as was seen very clearly in Al Ain.

Arnold clearly has a lot of work to do before the Socceroos take on Palestine in Dubai on 11 January.

* * *

The retirement from the game of Socceroos captain Mile Jedinak
left a gaping hole in the national team.

Jedinak, the quiet achiever with nerves of steel
12 July 2020

Socceroos legend Mile Jedinak, who announced his retirement from the game on Sunday, will be remembered as an exemplary captain with a fighting spirit and fierce determination to reach the top of his profession.

Throughout his career, Jedinak was an unflappable footballer with nerves of steel.

These latter qualities were no better illustrated than in a crucial FIFA World Cup match in Brazil in 2014.

The Socceroos were facing the mighty Netherlands in a Group B clash in Porto

Alegre and with the scores level at 1–1 nine minutes into the second half they were awarded a penalty after substitute Oliver Bozanic's attempted cross was handled by Daryl Janmaat.

With the weight of an entire nation on his shoulders, Jedinak was a beacon of concentration as he prepared to take the biggest kick of his career.

As thousands of Australians at the ground and millions of others around the world watched with bated breath, Jedinak nonchalantly sent goalkeeper Jasper Cilessen the wrong way and slotted the ball home with a low shot.

The Socceroos who dared to dream were on the cusp of greatness and as the entire squad were going berserk Jedinak simply raised his arm in muted jubilation and went straight back to his half to get on with things. The job was not done yet.

That was Jedinak to a tee.

Australia eventually lost 3–2 in a spellbinding thriller but the captain's strong influence on the side left nobody in any doubt about his stature as a player and a person.

And it is a fitting tribute to his personality that you will not find a bad word said about him from anyone in a career that started in Sydney's west and effectively ended on the biggest stage of all: the 2018 World Cup in Russia.

Jedinak, who will be 36 next month, played 73 full internationals and led the Socceroos to their first major honour when the Socceroos claimed an uplifting AFC Asian Cup triumph in 2015 on home soil.

The consistency he showed either in defence or in midfield for club and country throughout his career made him a most valuable and reliable asset to any coach lucky enough to have him under their wings.

Jedinak was also a handy dead-ball specialist, mind you.

He ended up scoring 18 goals for the Socceroos, ranging from a sweetly struck free-kick against Germany in a friendly in Kaiserslautern in 2011 to a hat-trick against Honduras in a World Cup playoff in Sydney in 2017.

Jedinak played with distinction for several clubs and he reached the peak of his ambition when he led Crystal Palace to the Premier League in 2013. He was voted the Londoners' player of the season.

In his first season in the premiership Jedinak's commitment to the cause was illustrated when he did not miss a minute's play in the entire campaign until he was injured in the last half hour of Palace's last match of the season.

No wonder Palace still regard him very highly. "A leader of men and club legend," was how the London club greeted his retirement.

Jedinak finished his career in 2018–19 with Aston Villa in the Championship, helping the Birmingham-based side secure promotion back to the Premier League.

One man who knows Jedinak very well is former Central Coast Mariners coach Lawrie McKinna.

Jedinak was a key player when the Mariners won the A-League Premiers' Plate in 2008 and McKinna, who is now Newcastle Jets chief executive, could not speak highly enough of his former protégé.

"Mile was driven to be a professional player since he was young," McKinna said.

"He became a great player, leader and role model. He also was and still is a very special person."

Jedinak's announcement of his retirement puts to bed any speculation that he could join the A-League next season.

The Global Scene

Hundreds of thousands of Australians are passionate followers of foreign football, thanks partly to SBS's commitment to bringing the world game to our lounge rooms in the early 1980s.

As Barcelona and Sampdoria prepared for the 1992 European Cup final at Wembley, the origins of the famous competition were brought to light.

Wolves, Fleet Street and the European Cup
19 May 1992

If Real Madrid made the European Cup such an instant hit with their marvellous football almost four decades ago, Wolverhampton Wanderers and the Fleet Street tabloids were the central figures behind the creation of the popular competition.

The famous Wolves of manager Stan Cullis, centre-half Billy Wright and centre-forward Roy Swinbourne were the best team in Britain in the early 1950s.

English football, however, was engulfed in a deep crisis at the time.

After losing to the United States in the first round of the 1950 World Cup, England were slaughtered twice by Hungary in 1953 and 1954 before they crashed to Uruguay in the quarter-finals of the World Cup in Switzerland.

Public morale was low and the game desperately needed an injection of confidence.

The morale booster came on a cold night at Molineux on December 13, 1954 when Wolves faced the magical Magyars of Honved Budapest in a friendly.

Wolves had already beaten Spartak Moscow 4-0 at home in another friendly a month earlier but Honved were a different proposition.

They went to the Midlands with a huge reputation and no fewer than five players who five months earlier had helped Hungary reach the World Cup final. The team included the dreaded Ferenc Puskas, Zoltan Czibor and Sandor Kocsis.

The midweek match under lights created enormous interest among British fans who were keen to watch these 'exotic' footballers who could play the game so well.

Honved's flawless, short-passing game left the partisan Molineux crowd spellbound in the first half.

But after racing to a two-goal lead, Honved were eventually swamped by the physically superior Wolves who scored two late goals to win an epic match 3-2.

The Wolves' performance captured the imagination of the disillusioned British public and Fleet Street did not miss such a glorious opportunity to drum up national pride.

All newspapers gave Wolves' triumph the coverage it so richly deserved but one headline in *The Daily Mail* may have changed the course and face of European football.

'Hail Wolves, champions of the world', it screamed, rather chauvinistically.

Gabriel Hanot, editor of the French sports daily *L'Equipe*, replied in an editorial: "We must wait for Wolves to visit Moscow and Budapest before we declare their invincibility. There are other teams in Europe who could lay claim to be the best in Europe, such as Real Madrid and AC Milan."

Hanot immediately drew up plans for a club competition for all the champion clubs of Europe to be played on a knockout, home-and-away basis.

It is history now how the first European Cup kicked off in 1955-56 and Real Madrid became the first winners of the trophy after they beat Reims 4-3 in Paris.

The European Cup today has become the biggest prize in world football and every club in the continent would dearly love to play in it, let alone win it.

When Barcelona and Sampdoria clash in this week's final at Wembley they will not only be fighting for the cup itself but also carrying on a great tradition set by the likes of Real, Milan, Ajax, Bayern Munich and Liverpool.

And when Ronald Koeman and Michael Laudrup, for Barcelona, and Sampdoria's Gianluca Vialli and Roberto Mancini step on the Wembley turf they will have to live up to the standards set by such greats as Alfredo Di Stefano, Eusebio, Gianni Rivera, Bobby Charlton, Johan Cruyff, Franz Beckenbauer and Marco Van Basten.

Such is the rich tradition of the European Cup.

Unfortunately, the financial rewards that go with the competition have often led managers and coaches to adopt an end-justifies-the-means approach to such finals.

Fortunately, however, a number of negative finals have failed to dampen the enthusiasm of the fans who still regard this as the biggest and highest-level competition in the world.

* * *

'QUOTE UNQUOTE'

The Socceroos' clash against Uruguay was fast approaching. With a World Cup spot on the line, this is what awaited them in Montevideo in late 2001.

Uruguay's sky blue blood ready to boil
16 November 2001

The boisterous crowd had been waiting fervently for the start of the match for two hours.

The terraces of Montevideo's old and historic Centenario Stadium were crammed with Uruguayan aficionados who were thirsty for Brazilian blood.

As the tension rose, the traditional war cry 'Soy Celeste' (I am a Sky Blue) reached a deafening crescendo.

Then, all of a sudden, the long wait was over.

Sixty-five thousand fans exploded into an unabashed frenzy when a few heads emerged from the players' tunnel and stepped on the field.

They were the ball boys.

When the two sets of gladiators actually came on to contest the 1995 Copa America final, the stadium became a sea of excitement and a coliseum of noise that made the 'Hampden roar' sound like a gentle whisper.

Smoke bombs filled the sky and firecrackers reverberated around the Centenario.

Brazil were being thrown to the lions.

This is the sort of reception Frank Farina's Australians can expect when they face Uruguay in the second leg of the 1998 World Cup playoff next weekend.

It will be Uruguay's biggest match since that sunny afternoon six years ago when they overcame their bitter rivals on penalties to capture South America's greatest prize.

Nothing has gone right for Uruguay since.

Los Celestes were knocked out in the first phase of the 1997 Copa America and were crushed in the 1999 final by Brazil before falling to Mexico in this year's semi-finals.

In between they even failed to reach the 1998 World Cup.

Although the country has done remarkably well to keep churning out star players from a limited field, it has been two decades now since Uruguay produced a genuine superstar like Enzo Francescoli, the man they called 'El Principe'.

The skinny forward, who could glide past opponents the same way as French ace Zinedine Zidane does today and who could mesmerise opponents with a ball at his feet, is but a distant memory to his many admirers in South America and Europe, which is where he spent most of his glittering career.

Coach Victor Pua today relies on the explosive left foot of Alvaro Recoba, the world's highest-paid player, to get his physical team past the Socceroos.

Recoba, 25, will return to Internazionale in December after serving a suspension for his involvement in the worldwide passports scandal.

He is a left-sided striker who has the ability to put his body between the ball and his opponent, which is something defenders hate because it is very hard to win the ball when you cannot see it.

However, Recoba is also terribly inconsistent and sometimes he can appear to be lazy but there are few players in the world who can hit the ball as venomously as he does from anywhere up to 35m.

Even by South American standards, the quality of his free kicks is such that Australia must not give away too many fouls anywhere near the penalty area because they would be asking for trouble. Big trouble.

The Uruguayans are hoping that this prolific striker nicknamed 'El Chino' for his oriental looks gets their side through to the finals for the first time since 1990.

It has been a long wait for Uruguay and their passionate fans. But, then again, they are used to it by now.

* * *

Football was the winner when Brazil lifted their fifth world crown in Japan. It was a privilege to be in Yokohama to watch Ronaldo's redemption.

Brazil profit from a licence to thrill
6 July 2002

Brazil, the charismatic kings of football, have exploded a few myths by snatching a fifth world title amid universal acclaim.

None more than the misguided perception that they had dumped their celebrated 'jogo bonito' in favour of a no-frills, safety-first approach.

Brazil won the 1994 World Cup with a minimum of thrills, raising fears that even the South American virtuosi had fallen into the temptation of putting results before style.

However, football's newest champions were the great showmen in Korea and Japan, entertaining the galleries with their attacking instincts that brought them goals galore.

Although the class of 2002 cannot be compared with that of the 'Beautiful Team' that conquered Mexico in 1970, the positive attitude of Cafu's samurai warriors was not dissimilar.

'QUOTE UNQUOTE'

Brazil won every match in 1970 with a brand of intoxicating football that left most rivals punch-drunk.

They had an unreliable keeper in Felix and a dodgy defender in Brito but for every goal they conceded they would score two or three.

The current defence was hardly a tower of strength—more like Fawlty Towers—and one could understand why Luiz Felipe Scolari's men always tried to play the game in the opposition's half, winning all seven matches in the process.

This fragile Brazil, in fact, will be best remembered for the prowess of strikers Ronaldo, Ronaldinho and Rivaldo.

The three Rs scored some of the carnival's finest goals, such as Ronaldo's cheeky toe-poke against Turkey, Ronaldinho's outrageous free kick against England and Rivaldo's sublime volley against Belgium.

Even erratic defender Edmilson showed enough co-ordination to find Costa Rica's net with a spectacular bicycle kick Pele himself would have been proud of.

Little wonder, then, Brazil enjoyed such massive support wherever they played, as was the case in Sunday's superb final against Germany in Yokohama.

The crowd was right behind Brazil and the roar that greeted Ronaldo's sweetly struck second goal nearly lifted the International Stadium's roof.

It was as if everyone felt the need to celebrate the uplifting redemption of a man who had suffered serious injuries but would not be beaten by adversity.

Many of us have a soft spot for a foreign team and Brazil's eye-catching style may explain why they have a special place in the hearts of millions of fans around the world.

But why are Brazil so successful?

The answer may lie in a curt explanation given by Scolari after the match.

"For us second place is never enough. Runners-up are losers," he said.

Clearly, moral victories are a myth in Brazil.

* * *

Fifty years after Hungary became the first visiting team to beat England, a seminal moment in football's history was revisited.

Magical Magyars cast a spell on Wembley
26 November 2003

The man who masterminded one of the finest victories in international football remembers very little of the match that made him and his country's football world famous.

Inside-forward and captain Ferenc Puskas was the biggest name in a troupe of 11 artists to don the cherry red jerseys of Hungary.

And on a foggy afternoon at Wembley on November 25, 1953, the 'Magical Magyars' created history by becoming the first non-British team to beat England on their home soil.

The Hungarians, playing in a novel 2-6-2 line-up as opposed to the common WM everybody seemed to use those days, gave Billy Wright's team a football lesson in a momentous match that sent shockwaves throughout the sporting world.

With No 9 Nandor Hidegkuti driving centre-half Harry Johnston crazy in his deep lying centre-forward role and the two wingers dropping back to strengthen midfield, England could not cope with the ball-playing Hungarians and were soundly beaten 6-3.

Hidegkuti helped himself to a hat-trick.

It was yet another magnificent all-round performance from a team that had not lost for more than three years and would reach the Word Cup final in Switzerland several months later.

Yet the moment that stuck in the memory of almost 100,000 spellbound Wembley fans for decades came after 24 minutes.

Hungary were 2-1 up when the portly Puskas controlled a pass in the six-yard box that came from left-winger Zoltan Czibor, who had lost right-back Alf Ramsey by veering to the right flank.

Puskas dragged the ball back with the studs of his boot as defender Wright charged in and ended up on the deck.

"Wright went past him like a fire engine going to the wrong fire" was how *The Times* described that jaw-dropping virtuosity.

Puskas completed the move by firing an unstoppable rising shot to the near post that found the net.

All this came from one mesmerising movement from his deadly left foot.

Puskas, 76, today suffers from Alzheimer's Disease.

Yesterday he caught up with some of his old mates at a function in Budapest commemorating the extraordinary event that revolutionised football.

But he stayed for only five minutes and had to go back to hospital.

One player who was in an ideal position to appreciate the skills of that very special team was goalkeeper Gyula Grosics.

"We went into the match with low spirits after drawing at home with Sweden in a friendly 10 days earlier," Grosics, 77, said via an interpreter yesterday.

"We would have settled for a draw or perhaps a narrow win so the 6-3 result caught us completely by surprise.

"The match was without doubt the highlight of my career and the memory will never fade away.

"We had a fantastic team centred on four great players: Hidegkuti, Puskas, Jozef Bozsik and Sandor Kocsis.

"They all had tremendous ability and a vast knowledge of the game."

With not a hint of modesty he added: "Our goalkeeper was not bad either."

As if to show that the Wembley result was no fluke, when the two national teams met again in another friendly in Budapest six months later the Magyars won 7-1.

* * *

Greece turned the football world on its axis by winning EURO 2004.
I was in Portugal to catch most of the action.

Gallant Greeks thumb their noses at orthodoxy
6 July 2004

The amazing events that took place at the Stadium of Light in Lisbon yesterday confirmed once and for all that football's world order is undergoing a seismic change.

And the game is all the better for it.

The 2002 World Cup will be remembered for its shock results and the way in which several superpowers were brought down to earth.

In the end, however, it was Brazil and Germany—the world's most successful football nations—that contested the Yokohama final.

The gallant Greeks yesterday turned the sporting world completely upside down by actually winning the European Championship after starting the tournament as rank outsiders.

A headed goal from striker Angelos Charisteas gave the Greeks a 1-0 victory over home side Portugal.

And the biggest shock of all was the competent way the 'Legends of Lisbon' did it.

Make no mistake, Otto Rehhagel's men did not pinch this trophy.

They won it fair and square and they thoroughly deserved it.

And they did it by beating holders France, hotshots Czech Republic and host country Portugal twice in the finest three weeks in Greek football history.

Quite extraordinary, when you remember that Greece had never ever won a match at a major tournament.

If this win proves anything it is that the game's establishment must accept the undeniable fact that nothing can be taken for granted anymore.

The gap between the haves and the have nots has never been narrower and Greece have proved this with stunning effect.

Many pundits, myself included, admired their bravery but did not expect them to go far.

Yet, to their eternal credit, Greece never flinched and as their incredibly organised defence got better and better, the team's confidence grew and in the end the players must have felt as if they could walk on water.

Much has been said about Greece's lack of adventure and how an overall Greek victory would not be too good for the game. What a load of rubbish!

The team, marvellously led by AEK midfielder Theodoros Zagorakis, won yesterday's final against Portugal simply because technically and tactically they were the better team.

Portugal's passes became hurried as the night progressed and too often the home side were forced to push the ball sideways rather than forward because there was no way through.

This of course played into Greece's hands and as the clock ticked it was becoming increasingly obvious that it was not going to be Portugal's day.

The rest is history, literally.

They will be talking for decades about the day Greece scaled football's Mount Olympus.

* * *

The 2006 Champions League final telecast was marred by a pro-English commentary and broadcaster SBS was forced into defensive action.

SBS vows to pull the plug on English bias
21 May 2006

SBS has promised to veto English feeds for major matches after Andy Gray's jingoistic Champions League final commentary.

The multicultural station, which prides itself on impartial reporting, admitted that it was deeply embarrassed by Gray's pro-English bias during the Barcelona-Arsenal showdown.

Gray's commentary on Sky was designed for a British audience but SBS should have made sure Australian viewers did not have to put up with such blatant bias.

Head of sport Les Murray said he was "unaware until the last moment that Sky's feed would include commentary from Gray".

"We took a risk with him but it won't happen again," Murray said.

"If an English team makes a major final, no way we'll take a feed from an English network.

"I had no idea Gray was going to be that bad."

One-eyed Gray also berated referee Terje Hauge for the rest of the game after the Norwegian rightly sent off Arsenal goalkeeper Jens Lehmann.

"This match is too big for this referee," an exasperated Gray said.

Judging by the poor quality of his call, a Champions League final might have been a wee bit too overwhelming for Gray too.

The game was billed as the 'Ronaldinho–Henry final' but the winner was … Samuel Eto'o.

The treacherous Cameroon striker stole the show in a dramatic match that lived up to expectation.

Spanish champions Barcelona owe their second Euro triumph to an exciting goal poacher who unfortunately won't grace the World Cup because his country did not make it.

African player of the year Eto'o was heavily involved in the game's decisive moments.

It was he who ran on to a peach of a pass from Ronaldinho to force keeper Lehmann to foul him and get sent off.

It was he who turned Sol Campbell beautifully to bring a fingertip save from Manuel Almunia.

And it was he who came from the blind side of Arsenal's defence to square the match with a placed shot to the near post.

Eto'o's contribution to his team's cause has earned him a special place in the hearts of Barca's legion of fans worldwide.

It also explains why Barca can be so irresistible on their day.

With Ronaldinho given very little time and space to weave his magic, the Brazilian ace was unable to leave a telling mark on the match.

Thankfully for coach Frank Rijkaard, Eto'o chose the big occasion to emerge from a scoring slump with deadly effect.

Yet Arsenal captain Thierry Henry, of all people, should have put the game beyond Barca's reach by taking a glorious chance midway through the second half when the Gunners were a goal ahead.

As he did in the first few minutes, Henry came face to face with Victor Valdes but shot straight at the goalkeeper's body.

* * *

A corruption scandal in Italy that broke on the eve of the 2006 World Cup threw the Italian game into turmoil.

Italian football: the seedy side of the world game
28 May 2006

Italy's World Cup aspirations have been dealt a massive blow by the escalating scandal that has leaders of the global game worried.

Phone tap disclosures of conversations involving top club officials and federal authorities have plunged this football-mad country into a crisis that seems to be getting bigger and more sinister every day.

Key players have said that the scandal was not affecting their preparation, even suggesting the worldwide indignation will serve as a motivator.

However, there is no doubt that this sordid mess has not come at an ideal time for the Azzurri.

"This is madness," FIFA president Sepp Blatter told Milan's *Corriere della Sera*. "How is it possible that Italian football has stooped so low? This is the greatest scandal in football history."

It all started when Turin prosecutors who were examining doping allegations at Juventus came across phone taps involving Juve general manager Luciano Moggi and referees commissioner Pierluigi Pairetto.

Milan's *Gazzetta dello Sport* has published the sensational transcripts.

Moggi, a man who wields enormous power in Italy and is seen as the 'Godfather' of Italian football, appears to have tried to influence Pairetto's refereeing appointments for Serie A matches involving Juventus.

Moggi is also being investigated over the modus operandi of player management company GEA, which is owned by his son Alessandro.

The inquiry is also dealing with allegations of widespread player gambling in Italy: AC Milan, Lazio and Fiorentina are implicated.

Juve's Gianluigi Buffon, arguably the best goalkeeper in the world, has appeared before Parma prosecutors to explain claims he bet heavily on matches.

Buffon protested his innocence, claiming he only bet on foreign football when it was legal to do so.

Socceroos goalkeeper Zeljko Kalac has also been involved.

A picture of the lanky custodian placing bets while on the books of Perugia was published in national papers.

Kalac, who now plays for Milan, has denied any wrongdoing, stating he only bets on horses.

The ongoing inquiry that centres on star players, referees, directors, government ministers, judges, police officers and even a television sports show host has thrown a huge question mark over the composition of the next Serie A championship.

If found guilty of match fixing, champions Juventus could have their 2005 and 2006 league titles rescinded and be demoted to Serie B.

The league also could be reduced to 16 teams.

UEFA is eager for the scandal to be resolved as quickly as possible and it would like to know if Italy is still willing to bid for the 2012 European Championships.

Juve, Milan and Fiorentina are supposed be playing in the next Champions League but if found guilty the three clubs could be ineligible to play in Europe.

Italy is a major football nation and this colossal mess has caused the world game huge embarrassment ... hence Blatter's deep concern.

So will this latest chapter in the long history of Italian football corruption affect the Azzurri's chances in the World Cup?

As with most things in Italy, it is probably anybody's guess, really.

* * *

The Football Association appointed Italian Fabio Capello as England coach after the 2006 World Cup. But the decision was seen by many as a huge gamble.

England's Capello marriage won't work
13 December 2007

The proposed marriage between England and 'no thrills' coach Fabio Capello is a disaster just waiting to happen if ever there was one.

When you remember the diametrically opposed cultures governing English and Italian football, such a strange partnership has 'un bel fiasco' written all over it.

Or 'a bloody mess', as the English would put it.

The English Football Association is expected to announce in the next 48 hours that the 61-year-old Italian is the new England coach.

Good luck to both parties. They will need it.

Capello is a respected coach with an impressive CV and a supreme opportunist who does not come cheaply.

He still regards the opportunistic goal he scored against England in a friendly international at Wembley in late 1973 as the highlight of his international career.

Picking up a rebound from goalkeeper Peter Shilton, he steered the ball home from close range to give Italy a 1-0 victory, their first ever win on English soil.

Coming only weeks after England had failed to qualify for the 1974 World Cup by falling to Poland, the sad loss forced the Poms to take a good look at themselves as their once feared football began its spectacular free fall down the world's pecking order.

Capello would find a similar scenario if he took over the plum job of England coach.

England's football has flattered to deceive in recent years and a top-notch coach with vast international experience is seen as the panacea to the country's well-documented ills.

But is Capello, the quintessential Italian coach, the right man for the job? And is England right for Capello, for that matter?

We are not talking here of an England team being in the hands of Sweden's Sven-Goran Eriksson, who hails from a country that can be as English as the English themselves, not least in the way it plays the game.

We are dealing here with a man who will always make sure of not losing a match before he even entertains any thoughts of trying to win it.

And a man who is obsessed with winning trophies, no matter how.

How this clinical attitude will sit with the debonair English mentality remains to be seen, although one would think that any silverware Capello might bring to England would be greeted wildly and unreservedly across the length and breadth of the nation.

Having said that, one wonders how long Capello's honeymoon will last and how the two parties in this intriguing flight of fancy would react to the first signs of turbulence.

This is the million-dollar question millions of frustrated England followers around the world would be asking as the FA deliberates on a decision that could shape the future of the game in the country.

This will be the toughest job in Capello's career, no question about that.

You see, while the English go into major tournaments *hoping* to win them, the Italians enter such events *expecting* to win them, regardless of whether they are good enough to do so or not.

Which is probably the most significant difference between the two football schools: Capello might be in for a bigger culture shock than he thinks.

* * *

On the 60th anniversary of the Superga crash that claimed the lives of 31 people, Torino are still regarded as one of Italy's finest teams.

The day Italian football died
5 May 2009

Sixty years ago Italy was plunged into deep mourning when news filtered through that the 'Grande Torino' football team had perished in an air crash.

On the way home from a friendly match against Benfica in Lisbon to honour retiring captain Jose Ferreira on May 4, 1949, the Fiat G-212 carrying the cream of Italian football encountered heavy weather and crashed into a church on the side of a hill at Superga, just outside Turin and only a few minutes from its destination.

On board were 18 Torino stars, amongst them famous inside-forward Valentino Mazzola, one of Italy's finest ever players and the father of Internazionale's 60s legend Sandro. None of the 31 people on board survived.

Torino were no ordinary team. They were unbeaten at home since 1945 and in season 1947–48 they scored 125 goals in 40 matches on their way to the Serie A title.

When disaster struck they were on course for a fifth straight championship, having a four-point lead with only four matches to go.

The football-mad Italians were in shock. When news of the crash spread across the country, the parliament in Rome was immediately suspended.

The tragedy was also big news across the continent. In the pre-European Cup days, there was little contact between major clubs but Torino and their all-star cast were well known and respected.

Torino were awarded the 1949 championship even though they insisted they complete their league fixtures with their youth team and two first-team players who did not make the ill-fated trip to Portugal: reserve goalkeeper Renato Gandolfi and defender Sauro Toma.

Their four remaining rivals also picked a youth team out of respect for the side that had brought a smile back to the country after the ravages of World War II.

Italy, who were world champions at the time, fielded 10 Torino players in the team that defeated Ferenc Puskas's Hungary 3–2 in 1947.

With the 1950 World Cup in Brazil coming up, the Italian Football Federation had a battle on its hands to come up with a competitive team to defend its world crown.

As it turned out the below-par Azzurri were knocked out of the competition in the first phase after losing 3–2 to Sweden.

Torino slid into a rapid decline after their 1949 title.

Ten years later they were relegated as crosstown rivals Juventus ruled the roost domestically.

A Serie A championship in 1976 raised hopes of a revival but that solitary success of striker Francesco Graziani's team turned out to be a false dawn.

The Granata had become very much the other team in Turin and spent most of the 1990s in the second division and even this year they are struggling to stay up.

The Torino stars who perished: Valerio Bacigalupo (goalkeeper), Dino Ballarin (goalkeeper), Aldo Ballarin (defender), Emile Bongiorni (forward), Eusebio Castigliano (midfielder), Rubens Fandini (midfielder), Guglielmo Gabetto (forward), Ruggero Grava (forward), Giuseppe Grezar (defender), Ezio Loik (defender), Virgilio Maroso (defender), Danilo Martelli (midfielder), Valentino Mazzola (forward), Romeo Menti (winger), Piero Operto (defender), Franco Ossola (forward), Mario Rigamonti (midfielder), Julius Schubert (midfielder).

* * *

Spanish giants Barcelona capped a magnificent year by winning the 2011 Club World Cup to establish themselves as one of the greatest sides in European history.

Barcelona is a club with no peer
19 December 2011

Barcelona's ability to consistently dismantle the world's finest teams on the biggest stages ranks them among the greatest sides ever.

Trying to find fresh superlatives to describe the quality of Barcelona's play is becoming a pointless and rather tedious exercise.

What else can you say and how much more can you rave about this Spanish matador that is torturing the world's finest teams into a slow death?

Most adjectives found in a thesaurus associated with the words 'beautiful', 'successful', 'inspiring' and what not will have been used ad nauseam to tell the story of a team that will be remembered as one of the greatest of all time.

If not the best ever, full stop.

Yet an aspect of their game that does not get as much publicity as it should is the fact that, contrary to several other successful sides, Barca are a team that love nothing more than to rise to the occasion.

The bigger the event, the better they play.

Choking certainly is not part of Barcelona's vocabulary.

Since Pep Guardiola took over the reins of the club in 2008, Barcelona have rewritten the game's record books.

In just over three seasons at the Nou Camp, Guardiola has masterminded two UEFA Champions League titles, three Primera Division championships and two FIFA Club World Cup trophies.

This is to go with a few extras like three European Super Cups, two Spanish Super Cups and one Copa del Rey.

In this golden period Barca have lost only one Champions League semi-final against Internazionale in 2010 and one Copa del Rey final to Real Madrid in 2011.

Which goes to show that, putting aside those two aberrations, one of Barcelona's greatest attributes is their capacity not to be intimidated by the big occasions but see them as an opportunity to satisfy an insatiable hunger for silverware.

This is a vital aspect that sets Barca apart from other great teams of the past.

Even Franco Baresi's AC Milan and Zinedine Zidane's Real Madrid, for all their undoubted class, were not immune to the occasional slip-up that cost them dearly.

Watching Barcelona crush Santos of Brazil 4-0 in the CWC final at the weekend reinforced the belief that when in the mood this team can make even the best of teams look pretty ordinary.

At the risk of being accused of Euro-snobbery, the Copa Libertadores is not as technically strong as the Champions League but the Brazilian side is nonetheless South America's finest and would have justifiably gone into the match with a degree of confidence.

But, same as they did to Manchester United in the UCL final in May, Barca chose the big stage to unleash their range of mesmerising football.

With world class trio Lionel Messi, Andres Iniesta and Xavi Hernandez in sublime touch, there was little poor Santos could do to stem the tide.

Barca will go back to Spain to resume their fierce battle with Real Madrid for the Spanish league title.

They might suffer the odd defeat here or there but one thing is as certain as night and day: when it comes down to the matches that matter most Barcelona will be up for them and ready to plunder.

* * *

Tens of thousands of German fans flocked to Wembley for the 2013 Champions League final between Bayern Munich and Borussia Dortmund. This was one of my reports from London.

English game grapples with winds of change
25 May 2013

One of London's most popular tourist attractions is the daily ritual of the changing of the guard at Buckingham Palace.

Hundreds of onlookers flock to the capital's world famous landmark every morning to see the ceremony of the exchange of guard duties.

Seven miles to the north west of the palace, European football will witness another changing of the guard when German giants Bayern Munich and Borussia Dortmund clash for the UEFA Champions League trophy at Wembley Stadium on Sunday morning (AEST).

England's Premier League and Spain's Primera Division have had a stranglehold on Europe's most important club competition for the best part of the last decade.

However, the winds of change that hit the continental game this season have turned into a gale force as the Bundesliga showed in no uncertain terms in two groundbreaking semi-finals that it is ready to rule Europe in the same way as it did in the 1970s.

While the Premier League lost all its representatives before the quarter-final stage and La Liga's Barcelona and Real Madrid were unceremoniously dumped in the semi-finals, Bayern and Dortmund marched on relentlessly and they will show an expected worldwide television audience of 150 million what German football today is all about.

The mood in London—the home of Arsenal, Chelsea and Tottenham Hotspur who have Euro visions—is one of apathy at worst or at best a realisation that the premiership has missed a great opportunity on the 150th anniversary of its Football Association.

As thousands of well-mannered fans from Bayern and Dortmund began pouring into the city and will converge on the Trafalgar Square fan zone if the weather permits, London and its media are not getting too excited about this final.

The windy, wet and freezing conditions that continue to batter London have nothing to do with it.

So far the media is giving the twin powers of Wembley and their stars less treatment than the comings and goings of premiership managers and players or the second cricket Test between England and New Zealand.

There is also next week's eagerly awaited Championship playoff between Crystal Palace and Watford.

Which is all perfectly understandable from an English perspective.

The overriding feeling, however, is that football fans in London either could not care less or are grudgingly taking a back seat to let Germany's elite enjoy 'Der Klassiker' at their expense.

Bayern are hot favourites to win their fifth continental crown but they need only to look back at last season's final against Chelsea in Munich to know how easily things can change in the rarefied air of football's highest level.

This will be Bayern's third UCL final in four seasons and it will be desperate to make up for two devastating losses to Internazionale and Chelsea.

Coach Jupp Heynckes has dismissed suggestions that his side is mentally brittle.

"No, I don't see that at all," he said this week.

"We are very strong mentally and psychologically. When you have lost the Champions League (to Chelsea) after being the better team for 120 minutes it takes some guts to recover from that."

Yet striker Thomas Muller also said it was important for Bayern to win the elusive trophy because the club would not take kindly to being labelled as "losers".

If you forget the general lack of English interest in the final fest, the last word should go to a ticket collector at an underground station.

After seeing a few Dortmund fans walk past him, he asked me, "Why do two German teams have to play each other over here in London? It's stupid."

There are some people—even in England—who do not understand how football works.

*   *   *

With defensive and negative tactics virtually eliminated from the game, the merits of the rule that made away goals count double were brought into question.

Does football still need the away-goals rule?
12 March 2017

Football's away-goals rule has served its purpose very well but it is time for the question to be asked if the game really needs it anymore.

The ruling was introduced by European governing body UEFA half a century ago and was trialled in the 1965–66 Cup Winners' Cup.

It was devised as a means of encouraging teams not to play defensively in away games.

It worked a treat as the prospect of scoring a goal that would count double if a knockout tie ended in an aggregate draw forced away teams to be less defensive and more adventurous.

The ruling was later extended to national teams and it is the way FIFA and UEFA playoffs are run.

But the game has changed dramatically since those dark days of the early 60s when defensive and negative football was rife.

Today the vast majority of teams are far less inclined to park the bus than they used to, essentially because the mentality of most football managers has changed.

Being defensive today is seen as old-fashioned and counterproductive: certainly a step backwards.

This is not to say that teams will not occasionally dabble with defence when they feel it is their best chance of success but they are the ones that probably would do so even if away goals counted treble.

Today's game is far more attack-minded and this positivity is ingrained in most sides at national and club level.

And the counter-attack is at the forefront of most clubs' or countries' modus operandi, whether they are playing at home or away.

In the 1960s counter-attacks used to be performed essentially by two or three men who got on the end of long passes from defence.

But today the teams that use this most effective of tactics flood the opposition with four or five men, using quick passing and movement to get from A to B.

This attitude is also helped by the fact that modern pitches are of the highest standard and they encourage attacking football because it is much easier to play out of defence than it used to be.

The rewards for attacking football are there for all to see.

So it is doubtful if today's teams would have a go in attack because of the reward of an away goal that counts double or due to the fact that attack is ingrained in their mindset.

There are many who regard the away-goals rule as cruel, unfair and even illogical. Remember, it was introduced as an artificial measure to combat catenaccio.

With catenaccio now effectively obsolete, you wonder if the rule is still as important as it used to be all those years ago.

Of course, the downside of abolishing away goals is that football would be faced with the increased likelihood of matches having to go to extra time with the prospect of the dreaded penalties.

But this is still the case when two teams cannot be separated after 90 or 120 minutes.

So why not take a drawn tie regardless of the scores into extra time and activate the away goals only if the extra 30 minutes do not provide a winner?

The cynic in me would suggest that teams that are 'ahead' on away goals could play for a draw in extra time, knowing that they would be awarded the tie. And this would defeat the purpose of the exercise, I suppose.

But the positive side tells me that this solution will rid us of a high proportion of games that are ruined by away goals, as could so easily have been the case when Paris Saint-Germain crashed spectacularly against Barcelona. PSG won the first leg 4–0 and lost the return 1–6.

Forgetting Barca's late, late rally that turned the tie in their favour, Edinson Cavani's away goal on the hour that made the score 3–1 seemed to have killed off the contest.

The atmosphere of the game changed. You could just see it in the body language of both sets of players and a fantastic football match was nearly reduced to a non-event between a team that 'knew' it was through and another that 'knew' it was out.

Without Barca's late heroics the match would have gone down as a quality contest that ended after 62 minutes.

There have been many cases of teams' dreams of glory being dashed by the gut-wrenching away-goals rule.

We in Australia should look no further than the extraordinary events surrounding the Socceroos' FIFA World Cup playoff against Iran in Melbourne in 1997.

The Iranians were on the receiving end of a constant barrage from the Socceroos that night and only went through to the finals because the law makers chose to make away goals count double.

It was not the first time and would not be the last time this happened.

* * *

The cultured city of Milan is not the football capital it used to be in its heyday and you could feel its decline by just walking in the streets.

Wounded Milanese duo rely on Chinese medicine
2 July 2017

As one of the great capitals of European football, the city of Milan continues to lick the deep wounds emanating from one of the darkest and most hurtful periods in its decorated history.

AC Milan and Internazionale are two of the giants of the world game but you would not know it by walking in the streets or visiting the bars of this stylish metropolis in northern Italy.

The city justifiably used to be very proud of its football—even cocky at times—but this does not seem to be the case anymore.

You can just feel the despondency, resignation and apathy in the air.

Fewer people engage in heated football conversations these days, the city-based papers seem to devote more space to other teams than their own and you are just as likely to see passersby wearing a Juventus, Napoli, Barcelona or Real Madrid jersey than one of Milan's two big clubs that have hundreds of thousands of followers around the world.

Milan and Inter have won 10 European Cup/Champions League titles between them and shared no fewer than 36 Italian championships.

Not so long ago, any ambitious player from anywhere in the world would have yearned to call the ageing but still fabulous Meazza Stadium at San Siro his home ground.

The Derby della Madonnina, so called for the golden statue of Our Lady that sits at the highest point of Milan's Duomo, used to be one of the most eagerly awaited fixtures of the European season, nearly up there with Spain's El Clasico between Madrid and Barca.

However, it has been seven long years since the blue and black half of the city had something to cheer about.

That is when Javier Zanetti's 'Nerazzurri' took a major step towards landing a magnificent Champions League, Serie A and Coppa Italia treble by beating Bayern Munich 2-0 in the 2010 final in Madrid.

Milan fans were able to celebrate an Italian league title a year later but they had to go way back to 2006-07 for a continental honour—when Paolo Maldini's 'Rossoneri' beat Liverpool 2-1 in the UCL final in Athens.

Subsequent years provided a litany of dismal debacles and colossal cock-ups as both clubs' common enemy Juventus became the undisputed leaders of the Italian game—winning the last six domestic championships.

As if this was not enough to illustrate that the famous football city clearly had lost its power and influence on the Italian game, regional side Atalanta from nearby Bergamo finished ahead of Milan and Inter for the first time in Serie A history and came fourth.

The two sets of disgruntled Milanese fans certainly are entitled to ask the 'George Best' question: where did it all go wrong?

Everyone in Italy has an opinion on Calcio—and the reasons for the gradual demise of Milan's glamour clubs are varied—but the most common one seems to be that the two organisations were let down by the two men who had made them great.

This also is the opinion of Paolo Condo, a senior columnist of Milan's *Gazzetta dello Sport*, the famous 'pink one'.

"Milan and Inter have rested on their laurels and they are now paying the price," Condo told me.

"Previous owner Silvio Berlusconi used Milan to boost his business empire and political aspirations but times have changed.

"The presidency of the 'first' Milan made Berlusconi very famous and successful but when he stepped aside and the 'second' Milan was ushered in, his sons did not have the same lofty objectives and aspirations.

"The football department of (parent company) Fininvest was seen as a little hobby in the general scheme of things and investments in players were drastically cut. The team naturally became less and less competitive.

"Berlusconi's political career has been in decline for several years so much so that for today's younger fans he was synonymous with failure—someone who could not attract top players anymore—and they were even glad to see the back of him."

Inter's situation was slightly different but it had the same disastrous outcome.

"Inter's previous multimillionaire owner Massimo Moratti, a petroleum magnate who inherited a fortune from his father Angelo, is from the old school of football club owners but his model based on massive outlays of his own money was antiquated," Condo said.

"This family approach does not work anymore in modern times. Today's biggest clubs are owned by economic empires or even sovereigns ... look at Paris Saint-Germain, for example."

The fans of the two clubs would have every right to feel frustrated but now that Milan and Inter are owned by wealthy Chinese groups there exists a glimmer of hope that finally the famous occupants of San Siro can live up to their name and become far more competitive on the domestic and foreign fronts.

Milan are now owned by Rossoneri Sport Investment Lux, a company linked to Chinese millionaire Li Yonghong, while Inter's new owners are the Nanjing-based Suning Commerce Group.

The two clubs face arguably the most important season of the next decade when Serie A kicks off in September.

With the Champions League eligibility rules amended to allow Italy four teams as from 2018-19 (as long as Serie A is ranked in Europe's top four), it is imperative that Milan and Inter secure a spot that would give them an opportunity to reap the massive financial rewards that await all participants, especially the most successful ones.

Milan and Inter are part and parcel of the European game and the city that has hosted some of football's finest and most memorable moments simply deserves better football than what is being dished out at the moment.

* * *

A sumptuous display from Lionel Messi in the Champions League consolidated his status as one of football's all-time greats. For me he is the greatest.

Why magical Messi is the greatest of all time
18 April 2019

The football world should bestow Lionel Messi with the highest accolade by proclaiming the Argentine wizard as the greatest player of all time.

There is no point in delaying the inevitable anymore so let's stop pussy-footing about this.

The man from the land of the tango has danced his way past mesmerised opponents and into sporting immortality with the way he has taken the game to a new level.

The world game's constituents were left gasping for breath after yet another master class from Messi this week.

Barcelona's superstar produced a dazzling all-round display against Manchester United to help steer his club to the UEFA Champions League semi-finals.

Messi scored twice and was heavily involved in another goal in a 3–0 romp and his man-of-the-match performance confirmed his unequivocal status as the best player in the world.

No one—not even Portuguese predator Cristiano Ronaldo, red-hot Egyptian Mohamed Salah or flamboyant Frenchman Kylian Mbappe—has the dribbling, passing and shooting skills to go with the vision, speed of thought and capacity to influence a game which the Argentine possesses in abundance.

Ronaldo, Salah and Mbappe might be on a par with Messi in an area or two but as a complete package they fall short.

The football fraternity certainly would be perfectly placed to give its verdict on whether Messi is indeed the greatest ever player.

I have maintained for a long time that Messi—for all his jaw-dropping brilliance—was still one step lower than a South American triumvirate that to me are football's all-time gods.

I refer to Brazil's Pele and Argentina's Alfredo di Stefano and Diego Maradona.

And, yes, I'm old enough to have seen all three in action many times.

However, since Messi keeps delivering at the highest level and is showing no signs of slowing down it would be impossible for anyone not to rate him as the greatest of all time.

He is at the peak of his mesmeric might at the moment.

What more does he have to do to convince the doubters?

Sceptics will point out that Messi cannot be considered the greatest unless he wins the FIFA World Cup.

But why should 'team' results influence the appraisal of an individual's qualities?

Was it Messi's fault that Gonzalo Higuain missed a sitter with the score at 0–0 in the 2014 World Cup final before Germany went on to win the trophy?

Was George Best deemed any less skilful because he came from Northern Ireland and never played in a World Cup or European Championship?

Others will say that playing for such a star-studded side as Barcelona carries a distinct advantage when it comes to establishing a player's pecking order.

Pele, Di Stefano and Maradona did not play their club football for battlers, did they?

Pele formed part of the great Santos side of the 1960s that dazzled the world with their 'exotic' football based on eye-catching individualism and eccentricity.

Di Stefano led the star-studded Real Madrid team that won the first five European Cups from 1956, scoring in every final.

And Maradona won two Serie A titles with Napoli at a time when Italian club football was the best in the world.

There is also the old adage about not comparing players or teams from different eras.

If we compare movies and film stars from different periods surely we can do the same with football.

With all respect, would the three stars of yesteryear have coped with modern opponents who are unquestionably stronger, faster and technically and tactically superior though not necessarily better to watch?

Of course, such views about the game's individual hierarchy are highly subjective ... based purely on taste, sentimentality and nostalgia.

And to a degree they are inconclusive and not designed to determine anything.

Yet, for all it's worth, I have no doubt anymore about football's hall of fame: Lionel Messi is the best and finest player I have ever seen.

* * *

Lionel Messi cut a forlorn figure as Barcelona were crushed by Bayern Munich in the Champions League, sparking speculation his days at the Camp Nou were numbered.

Barcelona and Messi do not deserve each other
15 August 2020

Lionel Messi must be feeling that 'enough is enough' and he should quit Barcelona and seek saner pastures after yet another painful illustration of how this chaotic club continues to fail him.

Messi was a sorry 'spectator' as Bayern Munich blitzed Barcelona 8-2 in an extraordinary UEFA Champions League quarter-final at the Stadium of Light in Lisbon.

The Argentine superstar would be entitled to fear that the lights have well and truly gone out at the once glorious club that has been in decline for a number of years.

Messi has given a lot to Barcelona and has been richly remunerated for his sublime efforts.

But the marriage has reached a stage where a divorce would benefit both parties.

The club would be able to start rebuilding without depending on the little Argentine to bail them out every other match and Messi would be in a position to win more trophies his stature as the world's finest player deserves.

Messi is in the third year of his four-year contract that is reportedly worth an equivalent of $900,000 a week and his get-out cause is $480 million.

While Messi continues to maintain his lofty standards, the ageing team he has carried for at least three years appears to have reached the end of the road.

And the club has a lot to answer for after consistently failing to supplement the team's formidable attacking power with enough quality and experience in defence and midfield.

Messi has not won the Champions League since 2015 and for a man of his quality that is not good enough.

On many occasions, he has seen his dreams of winning the most important trophy in world club football dashed by the sort of chaotic defending that made Barca easily beatable.

The rot started on the occasion of that 'historic' tie with Paris Saint-Germain in 2016-17.

Having lost the first leg 4-0, Barcelona turned the tables on PSG with a sensational 6-1 rout thanks largely to some benevolent refereeing that was conveniently overlooked in the euphoria surrounding one of football's epic comebacks.

Then came four consecutive eliminations that confirmed what everybody knew but few would highlight: the team was great to watch when going forward but was always liable to concede goals galore.

In that same UCL season Barca crashed in the quarter-finals after losing 3–0 to Juventus in Turin.

The following season they fell 3–0 to Roma at the Olimpico after they had won the first leg 4–1 and last season, after beating Liverpool 3–0 at Camp Nou, they crashed 4–0 at Anfield.

The Lisbon debacle has sent shockwaves around the world but, if the truth be told, the writing has been on the wall for Barca for at least three years.

Four embarrassing disasters is unacceptable for such an ambitious club that seems to have created an impression that it has more money than sense.

The club made several poor signings in the last few years in their quest to match Real Madrid at home and abroad and this failure must have left Messi a disappointed and dumbfounded figure.

The next few weeks will be interesting, no doubt about that.

The bottom line, however, is simple: Barcelona and Messi are not made for each other anymore.

*   *   *

Cristiano Ronaldo resumed his march towards immortality with another amazing display of scoring power. It was clear that the Portuguese predator would be remembered as the greatest scorer of all time.

Ronaldo is the greatest goal machine in history
9 September 2020

Cristiano Ronaldo's status in the hierarchy of the world game continues to be the subject of heated debate but there can be no question about his reputation as the finest goal scorer of all time.

You can argue all you like if the Portuguese superstar is or is not a better footballer than Argentina's Lionel Messi. It's a matter of opinion, after all.

But when it comes to facts and figures—and how they were attained—Ronaldo would have to be regarded as the game's deadliest goal machine in history.

His two splendid strikes against Sweden in the UEFA Nations League took his tally from 165 full internationals to 101 and made him the first European to reach a century of goals.

This phenomenal tally complements the 450 goals he scored in his club career that took him from Sporting Club to Juventus via Manchester United and Real Madrid.

His club and country total of 551 goals from 742 matches gives him an average of .74 goals a match ... that's three goals for every four matches over a period of 18 seasons.

Ronaldo's 101 strikes for the national team take him to within eight goals of Iran hero Ali Daei's 109 from 149 matches.

Portugal's talisman should surpass Daei's tally in the coming season but he does not need to do so to be seen as the greatest of all time.

Daei will always be remembered as one of Asia's most formidable strikers who spent most of his career in Iran and the Middle East, except for five seasons in Germany where he scored a less impressive 19 goals in 107 matches for Arminia Bielefeld, Bayern Munich and Hertha Berlin.

With all respect to Asian football, however, I'm sure that most reasonable fans would recognise the level of difficulty surrounding Ronaldo's feats when assessing the merits of both strikers.

It's a bit like saying Australia is a better footballing country than Scotland because it regularly qualifies for the FIFA World Cup while the Scots hardly ever make it.

I'm sure Scotland would dearly love to swap their qualification process with that of the Australians.

Brazilian duo Romario and Pele, and Germany's Gerd Muller, might have something to say about the suggestion that Ronaldo is the top man when it comes to scoring goals.

Romario's aggregate of 364 goals in 518 matches gives him an average of .70 goals a match which is not too inferior to Ronaldo's.

Pele's total of 618 goals from 652 matches gives him an average of .94 goals a game but doubts have emerged over the validity of some of the matches he played in. And 'O Rei' was a better overall player, anyway, and cannot really be regarded as a goal scorer.

Muller netted 555 times in 617 matches for an average of .89 goals a game but a portion of his club goals came in pre-Champions League days when Bayern Munich often met easy pickings in the first rounds of the competition.

Ronaldo never had such a luxury and he earned every goal he has scored, at least at club level.

Ronaldo does not do tap-ins and his brace against the Swedes that gave the Nations League holders a 2-0 victory in Stockholm perfectly illustrated his mastery of the ball when it comes to sticking it into the net.

In the first half he took a free kick three metres outside the penalty area and effortlessly floated the ball over the wall and it dipped past the outstretched arm of goalkeeper Robin Olsen.

It was vintage Ronaldo—"it does not get better than this", one commentator said. Well, it did, with 20 minutes to go.

Receiving a square ball from Joao Felix on the edge of the box he looked up and nonchalantly poked the ball over Olsen's body and into the far corner of the net as if he was at training having a bit of fun.

It was a sublime goal that smacked of positive arrogance and supreme confidence in his ability.

I do not think the world has seen or will ever see a more relentless scorer than Ronaldo.

Australian coach Frank Arok (L), seen here talking with Steve Maxwell at a training session in 1986, died in Serbia in 2021.

Adrian Alston says the "biggest mistake" in his career was opting for Luton Town after the 1974 World Cup, rather than Hertha Berlin.

René Higuita known as 'The Madman' played for the Colombian national team on 68 occasions. He visited Australia in 1995, the year after the worst year of his life.

Maradona (Argentina) leaves Claudio Gentile (Italy) on the ground in the group match at the 1982 World Cup. Italy won 2-1 and went on to win the tournament.

Prolific England striker, Gary Lineker, says he was "frozen out" of the squad by manager Graham Taylor in 1994. He is seen here at the England training camp ahead of the 1986 World Cup in Mexico.

Greece - the unlikely European champions of 2004.

Lionel Messi of Barcelona shares a laugh with manager Pep Guardiola after the UEFA Super Cup match Barcelona v FC Porto, August 2011.

Terry Venables had short spell as coach of Australia from 1997-1998, failing to qualify the team for the 1998 World Cup when they drew 2-2 to Iran in the final qualifying match.

Socceroos captain Lucas Neill with coach Pim Verbeek in 2009.

Mark Bosnich was one of Australia's finest goalkeepers with a career that included Aston Villa, Manchester United and Chelsea. He returned to play in Australia for a four-match stint with the Central Coast Mariners in 2008.

Ange Postecoglou, then coach of Australia, at what would be one of his last media conferences in that role before he sensationally resigned after steering the Socceroos through to qualification for the 2018 World Cup.

Italy had numerous problems off the field in 2006 but it didn't stop them winning the World Cup that year.

Adelaide United's 3-0 victory over Bunyodkor in the Asian Champions League in 2008 was seen as a "divine performance".

Socceroos and Leeds United teammates Mark Viduka and Harry Kewell in a Premier League game vs Birmingham City, 2002 – considered by many as two of the best players produced by Australia.

Brazilian legend and coach of Japan, Zico, looks on as Australia defeats Japan in their opening group game of the 2006 World Cup. Before the game, he had declared Japan was "out to get" Australia.

The A-League

The country's first fully professional league provided many highs and lows since its much-anticipated launch in 2005. Yet, despite all the odds, the A-League has become part of Australia's sporting landscape.

Sydney FC manager Terry Butcher had one simple warning for his players as they prepared to defend their A-League title: Diving is out.

Butcher wages war on divers
16 July 2006

Sydney FC coach Terry Butcher has warned his players that he detests diving and he won't tolerate cheating.

"Two dives and you're out," is the motto of the former England World Cup star, who has replaced German legend Pierre Littbarski at the helm of the A-League's first champions.

As football tries to come to terms with an aggressive cancer that's eating away at the game's credibility, Butcher declared that divers were cheats and had no place in his squad.

"Diving is not acceptable, I detest it," Butcher, 47, said as he prepared his team for their first match of the season, against Queensland in the Pre-Season Cup, last night.

"The overriding factor from this World Cup is that cheats do prosper. It's ironic that Italy's Fabio Grosso, who dived for the late penalty against Australia, scored the first goal in the semi-final and then put away the winning penalty in the shootout in the final.

"Even the penalty in the final was no penalty. Florent Malouda's dive was disgraceful. Football's a man's game and a player should stay on his feet for as long as possible. That's the Aussie way, too.

"I've already told my players that I don't like that. It's something that sticks in my throat.

"If one of my men dived to win a penalty, I would not be happy about it even though, as a coach, winning is important.

"I want to win games fairly and by being the better team.

"Obviously I would not drop an offender after one instance—that would be too harsh—but I would have a word with him for sure and ask him not to do it again."

Butcher had four successful years as Motherwell manager before he accepted the job in Australia, which he regards as a "huge challenge".

"Pierre set a very good standard here," Butcher said.

"A new team, a new club and a new league; winning it was a huge achievement and this year we aim to win the league again.

"Of course, I'm under pressure to produce but pressure doesn't worry me. I've had it all my life.

"We have the right players to do it, without a doubt, and Sydney fans can be assured they won't see the route one game because we will play passing football.

"There will be times when we will have to clear our lines and get the ball out of the box but making a 60m pass does not make it a long ball … it's a long pass.

"All I want from my fans is to give me time to prove that Sydney FC are a good passing team that can play the right way, with quality.

"The bottom line is winning but there are ways of winning and I'd like to win with a bit of style and panache."

Some observers said Sydney's choice of Butcher as their coach was ill advised, claiming he represented an old-fashioned English method.

But Butcher, the man who never ran away from a challenge as an uncompromising defender in the 1980s and as an ambitious young manager, has asked for Sydney's fans to give him a go before making any judgement.

"People are well entitled to their opinion but the criticism is not fair," Singapore-born Butcher said.

"They might argue that the English team has not done much in the past 40 years but the English club scene is healthy.

"Many premiership managers are foreign but the nucleus of most teams is English.

"I don't think there is anything wrong with the English game or with English coaches and anybody who has seen my teams play will realise that they will always want to play football first."

So what can Sydney fans expect from their team this year?

"Total commitment," Butcher emphasised.

"My players will want their fans to go away with the belief their heroes had given everything … and done it with style."

* * *

Craig Johnston, who quit Australia as a teenager to carve a successful career in England, said he was deeply impressed by the overall quality of the fledgling A-League.

Johnston 'shocked' by home improvements
11 February 2007

Newcastle football's favourite son Craig Johnston yesterday revealed he would have stayed in Australia and played for the Socceroos if the game was as healthy in the 1970s as it is today.

Johnston, who blazed a trail for dozens of Aussie players by leaving home to sign for Middlesbrough as a 16-year-old, yesterday said he was amazed by the giant strides being made by the new Australian game.

Johnston went on to become a decorated star with Liverpool, where he spent seven golden years from 1981.

However, two appearances for England's under-21s made him ineligible for Australia.

"You know what, if football in the '70s was as good and as well organised as it is today, I definitely would have stayed here," Johnston said.

"And I would have made myself available to play for Australia, no worries.

"The current level of organisation was never there and the playing standard is much better and so is the level of management.

"Every aspect of the game has improved, actually."

Johnston urged young Aussies with stars in their eyes to think "twice, three times" before leaving Australia for Europe.

"These days Aussie players have the right coaching and infrastructure that did not exist in my time," Johnston said.

"They've never had it so good so they should stay in Australia for as long as possible and develop their skills before they take the big step."

Johnston last week was at the Newcastle Jets versus Sydney FC semi-final second leg and said he could not believe what he saw.

"I was absolutely amazed—almost shocked—with everything to do with going to a football match in Australia," he said.

"The pitch was fantastic—very well kept—and even the new stand made the whole thing look very professional.

"Soccer was never like this since my days at the International Sports Centre.

The game was always seen as being amateurish because it had amateur facilities.

"The 24,000 crowd was very passionate, worth a goal start.

"I was impressed by the technique and ball control, particularly Newcastle's.

"Their attitude was outstanding although I was really shocked by the way Sydney capitulated.

"I actually felt sorry for Sydney's travelling fans, who had every reason to be upset with their team.

"But all in all it was a thoroughly enjoyable evening and the fans certainly got their money's worth.

"I've seen a few A-League matches on television and I'm hooked. It's good entertainment."

* * *

Socceroos goalkeeper Mark Bosnich was never far away from the headlines and the return to Australian football of the 'loveable larrikin' created huge interest.

Bozza revels in second chance
28 July 2008

Mark Bosnich was up to his flamboyant best when he thrilled the fans and the media on a wet and miserable day in Gosford on Sunday.

The former Socceroos goalkeeper is not the type of guy who uses such gatherings to dish out the usual plethora of clichés and inane excuses.

Bosnich, 36, is making a comeback to professional football after a lapse of seven years and he is smart enough to give the avaricious media what it wants.

With one major difference. When Bosnich talks he makes sense and he means what he says, too.

Running through the tape recording of his conference at the end of the Central Coast–Sydney FC Pre-Season Cup match at the weekend, it was easy to see why good old Bozza remains such a popular personality.

Eighteen minutes of tape revealed not only the flamboyant, exuberant and cocky nature of this great character but also his doubts, inhibitions and a deep appreciation of the fortune of getting a chance to redeem himself from his dark past.

The Mariners have given him the number 40 jersey which is quite appropriate: life begins at 40 for Australian football's lovable larrikin.

"Sorry, I'm late. I had my blow-dryer today," he told the waiting media contingent, looking a million dollars in a charcoal suit and with a wide grin to match. "Is the tie straight?"

Having broken the ice so smoothly—although with Bozza this is never really necessary—the goalkeeper talked about the 'big step' he made in his first competitive match in seven years although he admitted it was too early to tell if his comeback was on track to succeed.

The conversation soon turned to the 'butterflies in the belly' he was feeling before his first match on Australian soil since 1999.

Bosnich overcame his nerves with aplomb, keeping a clean sheet and even saving a penalty.

He was clearly loving every moment of the adulation but he also was quick to express his gratitude to all those around him who made his weekend debut such a great success story, not least his two central defenders 'Pedj (Bojic) and Wilks (Alex Wilkinson)'.

He mentioned radio's Alan Jones, Mariners coach Lawrie McKinna and his assistants, goalkeeper coach John Crawley and even the kitman without whose help 'this would not have been possible. You always have to have that at the back of your mind. For once I'm feeling very humble'.

Bosnich also said he was encouraged to learn that he could still handle high balls quite competently, even though the balls here in Australia tend to fly, he said.

"A mark of a good goalkeeper in my opinion is the way he dominates his box," he explained.

"They say that the older you get you discover that you are not able to come out for high balls as much as you were able to when you're younger.

"I was very happy with the way I dealt with pressure situations today. With shot-stopping you could be lucky but with crosses you have only a split second to make a decision and you could be made to look very foolish.

"However, it's a long way to go. I've still got a bit of weight to lose. I'm serious about this and I want to challenge for a place in the side when the league starts."

Bosnich by now had the gathering in the palm of his hand but when asked if he thought he was lucky to be getting another chance at life after his drug and personal problems he opened up even more.

"Of course I'm lucky," he said.

"People should count themselves fortunate to wake up in the morning and feel healthy.

"I think many people have someone in their family who has been through some health scare or even worse and that's when you put things into perspective.

"You only have to switch on to the nightly news to see how lucky we all are.

"My problems basically were self-inflicted and I was very lucky to be able to stop what I was doing.

"Family is very important in any walk of life and should not be taken for granted but for a while I veered away.

"My sister has three young children who look up to me and that showed me how important it is to behave yourself.

"I've also got a responsibility now to the younger players in the Mariners team.

"After what happened in the past and feeling so low for so long this (what happened today) does wonders for you."

So what's his immediate goal?

"Looking good. I like looking good and fit and healthy," he said.

Oh yes, the old Bozza is back, all right!

*   *   *

Adelaide United surged to the AFC Champions League final in 2008 thanks largely to an uplifting performance at Hindmarsh Stadium.

The night Vidmar got the better of Zico
9 October 2008

Adelaide United's incredible victory over Bunyodkor in the first leg of the AFC Champions League semi-final will go down as one of the great nights of Australian football.

The City of Churches had never seen anything like it. Nor had Australian club football.

Jam-packed Hindmarsh Stadium rocked to its foundations.

Adelaide did themselves and their country proud with a divine performance that bordered on fantasy football.

The proud Reds crushed Uzbekistan's champions 3–0 to take a commanding lead going into the return leg in Tashkent.

They were inspired by a superlative Cassio, who made two goals for Diego and Fabian Barbiero and earned the late penalty that may have sealed the tie.

They are now quite entitled to dream of becoming the first Australian club to win the ACL.

And on this evidence who would bet against them?

But that's only part of the story. If Adelaide go on to reach next month's two-legged final against Gamba Osaka or holders Urawa Reds, who drew 1-1 in the other semi-final, they would qualify for the rich Club World Cup in Japan in December regardless of whether they win the ACL.

And the man poised to mastermind the Reds' surge across Asia is none other than young coach Aurelio Vidmar.

The former Socceroos striker is very much an apprentice in terms of football coaching. And he was up against a master in former World Cup legend Zico.

"I'm flattered," Vidmar, 41, said when told that the Brazilian had complimented him for his team's performance.

"Zico was one of my childhood heroes. He was a fantastic player, a great midfielder. He was in the Brazilian team throughout the 80s that were just fantastic to watch.

"But he's got many more years in front of me. This is only my second year as a coach and I would like to stay in the game for a long time."

Vidmar showed on Wednesday night he was poised to become one of Australia's finest young coaches not so much for the emphatic if flattering 3-0 win but for the way he changed things around after a shaky start.

Bunyodkor were marginally the better and more positive team in the first half but Adelaide came into the picture when they started playing longer balls with a more direct approach to which the Uzbeks had no answer.

Zico did not have a plan B and some of his players' heads seemed to drop after midfielder Barbiero scored the second goal with 15 minutes to go.

So the apprentice came out on top in a fascinating confrontation between two clubs that almost had no right to be playing on the same pitch. They certainly are not on a level playing field.

The Tashkent club formerly known as Kuruvchi has been transformed since it was taken over by rich moguls this year.

They came to Australia from Tashkent with a 30-member squad led by $9m-a-year superstar Rivaldo, travelling in comfort on a charter flight.

Adelaide will have to get by with economy travel on scheduled flights and pull a few strings "just to get out of the airport", as Vidmar put it.

"We certainly will be backs to the wall when we start travelling again," Vidmar said.

Somehow one gets the feeling that Adelaide, who are so close to a major international final, won't be too bothered with the long flights any more.

* * *

'QUOTE UNQUOTE'

Adelaide United were soundly beaten in the 2008 AFC Champions League final and sections of the mainstream media took the opportunity to attack the game.

Anti-football mafia strikes again
15 November 2008

Australia's 'anti-football mafia' was at it again after Adelaide United's capitulation in Asia, raising old suspicions over the media's agenda.

As soon as our game hits some turbulence in its flight towards stability and respectability in a country that has acquired worldwide notoriety for football-bashing that goes back decades, 'Cosa Nostra' swings into action.

The scene for the latest episode of the mafia's angst was set when Adelaide United crashed to Gamba Osaka in the AFC Champions League final. It was a glorious opportunity to take a cheap shot at football.

The Reds from South Australia were guilty of a colossal capitulation to the Japanese side that showed us how real football should be played, it was claimed.

The Daily Telegraph columnist Rebecca Wilson did not take kindly to this perceived embarrassment Adelaide caused Australian sport on the international stage.

In the same week as Australia was staging some Mickey Mouse non-event preposterously called the rugby league world cup—the lower case 'w' and 'c' are not an oversight—Wilson came up with a scathing attack on the poor standard of football in this country.

You see, it is not in the interests of that game for boofheads called rugby league or that silly game called Aussie rules that football in Australia keeps improving.

In an indignant plea for the game to lift its standards, Wilson pontificated that the game was in crisis and getting nowhere with its below-standard national competition. She also raised doubts over the wisdom of increasing the league's size when there are so few decent players around.

Why can't we play like the Japanese, she implied, without realising that Adelaide had already beaten J.League champions Kashima Antlers in the quarter-finals.

But what really made me choke on my breakfast on Saturday was the grim realisation that Wilson's views were not necessarily wrong.

My problem with the poisonous article, which said absolutely nothing new by the way, was its tone, timing and motives behind it.

Regular readers of this website would know that it is not the first time that I've expressed grave concern over the general standard of the A-League that leaves a lot to be desired.

We all know that the A-League is still in its infancy and needs far more resources to even start competing with the money-laden Japanese clubs.

We all know that the game in Australia is fighting to overcome age-old perceptions created by a vitriolic and nervous media that has a lot to lose if football reaches its full potential here.

We all know that our Socceroos face stiff competition just to be in the top 50 in the world.

And we all know that most young players in this country can't wait for a chance to play in the bright lights of the European leagues for very obvious reasons.

So Wilson's rabid rant did not tell us anything we do not already know.

It just showed once again that some people still cannot accept football within Australia's sporting landscape. They pretend to like it when it suits them and then stick the knife in when something goes wrong.

Instead of feeling proud of the way Adelaide, in true Aussie style, punched above their weight during the whole competition to storm into an impossible final against Gamba, Wilson chose this occasion to vent her anti-football spleen and vitriol.

Her despicable attitude reinforced the belief that some people within Australia's media would not be too displeased with Australian football's failures abroad.

You learn to treat such biased and immature journalism with the contempt it so richly deserves.

Quite frankly, such people are becoming less relevant and are seen as old-fashioned writers who are still clinging to the past to protect their future. Wilson's misguided and narrow-minded views should be treated accordingly.

But for those who might believe what they read in the papers, especially influential ones like the Tele, let it be known that football is on the case and it does not need such blinkered journalism to be shown what needs to be done to raise its standards.

So the message to any surviving members of the anti-football brigade out there is: Don't you worry about football, we'll solve our problems on our own and in our own time.

* * *

'QUOTE UNQUOTE'

The locally based Socceroos' humbling home defeat to Kuwait in an AFC Asian Cup qualifier highlighted the unsatisfactory standard of the A-League.

Is the A-League as good as we think?
10 March 2009

It's about time we stopped pretending that the A-League is the best thing to hit our sport since Guus Hiddink.

The competition is going all right and the main thing, I suppose, is that it has survived in a difficult market and next season will have two new teams.

But the overall standard of play leaves a lot to be desired and the time has come for change.

The most embarrassing aspect of the A-League Australians' clash with Kuwait last week was not the humbling 1–0 defeat that came out of the blue.

The side of the game that hurt most was the way a bunch of semi-professionals and amateurs ranked 98 places below Australia went about what must have been a tough away match for them with an attitude of 'let's play football and see what happens'.

And, boy, didn't the men in blue show up the cumbersome Australians, whose play reminded us of the days when we used to be outplayed and outclassed by touring teams before we pinched some 0–0 draw and then claimed a moral victory on the basis of having created a couple of half chances.

Kuwait showed us that our game is unappealing, unimaginative, pedestrian and predictable, and some of our players lack the necessary skills to play representative football.

Newcastle Jets and Central Coast Mariners, Australia's ambassadors in this year's AFC Champions League, enter the competition with this backdrop and it will be interesting to see if they can emulate Adelaide United who reached last year's final against Gamba Osaka.

This season's ACL should tell us if the Reds' surge was accidental or a true reflection of the A-League's standard.

The Canberra match was a microcosm of the A-League: vigorous, muscular play with little thought and even less flair to back it up, an attacking mindset that is not supported by creative passing in the last third of the field and a 'hope for the best' long-ball approach when patience runs out.

While Australia huffed and puffed in search of an opening that never came, the Kuwaitis showed composure and mastery of the ball from the first whistle and actually played their best football when they were under pressure.

This is not the first time that a Socceroos match involving A-League players has received an unflattering report card.

Remember China, who gave the domestic Socceroos a football lesson in Sydney in their last match of the previous phase of World Cup qualifying?

Fans are entitled to wonder how long it is going to be before we realise that our style of league football is tactically antiquated and we are being exposed by countries that are ranked below us.

Or when we are going to bite the bullet and import a few foreign coaches to give our competition a breath of fresh air.

Football Federation Australia gets a bit twitchy when the standard of the A-League is brought into question.

Yet the FFA cannot remain in denial when the evidence suggests that the domestic game is clearly stagnant because overall standards are not rising.

And the reason they are not improving is because our style of football from grassroots upwards is still centred too much on raw physique and too little on subtle technique.

Australia's domestic football might score the odd international success which could be the result of various circumstances, not least our innate fighting spirit.

Adelaide's run to the 2008 ACL final was a case in point.

The Reds fought bravely against all odds, showing true Aussie grit and producing a magical half an hour in the semi-final against Bunyodkor that will go down in football folklore.

But in the competition's decisive match they were outclassed by Gamba essentially because the Japanese play a much better and more refined type of game.

Watching football in Australia today is an infinitely more exciting and rewarding experience than it used to be, not least because we are now involved in Asia and facing all the stiff challenges this vast continent is presenting us.

Even the A-League has an open, pleasant feel about it.

Most games are fiercely contested yet thankfully gamesmanship is virtually non-existent.

But unless we learn to play with far greater technique and more modern tactics, our long-term prospects for success abroad won't improve.

The Kuwaitis impressed a healthy gathering at Canberra Stadium with their first touch and their ability to pass the ball with intelligence to players who ran into space with intent.

Australia could have stolen an undeserved draw in the end but in reality they should have lost by more than one goal.

It took a double humiliation by Hungary (6–3 at Wembley and 7–1 in Budapest) in 1953 for the English to take a good look at the mirror and realise that they were deluding themselves with their archaic 'made in England' football.

The Poms were forced to modernise their game. They did so, perhaps even reluctantly, but 13 years later they won the World Cup.

An unequivocal disaster on the international stage might just be what the A-League needs for change to take place.

* * *

News Limited was forced to defend its contentious coverage of the game after another incident of football bashing angered many fans.

News Ltd refutes accusations of bias
21 June 2009

News Limited's sport hierarchy has strongly defended its perceived anti-football bias among supporters of the world game.

The Socceroos have just qualified for their second straight World Cup, Australia has launched a bold bid for the 2018 or 2022 World Cup and the fifth A-League starting shortly is preparing to welcome two new teams.

Yet the overall mood of the fans at large is not as exhilarating as it should be. A lingering degree of anger and sense of injustice lies just beneath the surface.

The reason for this despondence is that the game has received a bit of a hammering from sections of the media in the last few weeks.

Whether it's the Socceroos' style of play, the controversial attitude of national coach Pim Verbeek, the standard of the A-League or now the Tim Cahill Case, football has had to endure a constant, vitriolic attack from the media.

News Limited, as publisher of *The Daily Telegraph* and *The Sunday Telegraph*, has been in the forefront of this and not surprisingly has come in for plenty of criticism for its perceived bias against the game.

But are the fans right? Executive sports editor Phil Rothfield kindly accepted our invitation to defend the two papers in a frank 'question and answer'.

Football has made great strides forward the last few years in its bid to rid itself of its dark past. What's your view of the game's image and its position in Australian sport's landscape?

"The game has made unbelievable progress since the last World Cup. They've launched the A-League which is a very good competition for what it is. I've been to a couple of games and I've enjoyed the family atmosphere. The game has done very well but I still think there are a lot of problems behind the scenes that a few people in soccer are not prepared to address."

There is a perception among football fans that News Limited, particularly The Daily Telegraph *and* The Sunday Telegraph*, has an agenda because it is not in the interest of the organisation that football keeps rising in this country. What do you say to that?*

"I deny an agenda against the game at all. If you see Saturday's paper, Andrew Webster went down to see Frank Lowy and wrote a positive piece in a double page spread about the FFA chairman's passion and hopes of delivering the World Cup to Australia. I have known Ben Buckley for a long time and I speak to him probably three, four times a year. I presume you are referring to the Tim Cahill story when you suggest we have an agenda against soccer."

No, not at all, the Cahill story is only one of many over the years.

"I honestly believe the Cahill affair has been a cover-up from the FFA. We spoke to the head of security at the Trademark Hotel that night who confirmed that there was a very serious incident there. Look, we are not here to look after the public relations of any sport. There is one problem I do have with soccer in Australia. I believe many soccer writers in this country see themselves as the guardian angels of the game. They are very reluctant to tackle officials when there are problems."

But the whole gist of the story is based on the claims of an unnamed witness and bouncer. Both allegations have been blown out of the water by the night club's management.

"I don't know about the story being blown out of the water. I've had several calls from people who are in the know who claim staff were threatened at the night club. And to be honest I think the night club has covered it up and so has the FFA. This guy who has been a head of security at Kings Cross for many years is not going to make up the story. The headlines about the whole thing are not what football fans want to read every day. Look at the scrutiny rugby league and cricket players are under. When we sign up to be journalists we have a responsibility to search for the truth and tell the full story to the best of our ability and not just write about Cahill scoring two goals. That's all we're doing."

Yes, but The Daily Telegraph *had a heading to a story saying 'Cahill banned from club' on the basis that the bouncer merely said he was not welcome at the club. That's hardly being banned, is it?*

"Look, I've checked this with the head of security. His name is Dave Millward. They told me Cahill would not be welcome as long as his bouncers were at the door. He would not get past the door if this guy is on duty."

So why was this not written into the story?

"Well, it's the same thing, isn't it ... being unwelcome and being banned."

Not really.

"Well, I read it as being banned."

Football people get a good coverage from Fox, SBS and Fairfax. Why would any football fan buy the Tele, whose coverage of the game is at best unsatisfactory?

"I genuinely believe that we have the best soccer coverage of the main newspapers in Australia. Just because we don't publish what the FFA wants us to print all the time doesn't mean our coverage is unsatisfactory. The most passionate of fans might agree with what you're saying but I can assure you that the general public—and I'm not here just to put out a paper for soccer fans—gets a fair coverage of the game. Last year we had three soccer writers and you've done a bit of work for us too."

Yes, but for all the space you give football, one cadet journalist would have been enough, wouldn't it?

"No, I disagree with that. By the way, you keep referring to the game as 'football'. Why are the Socceroos not called 'Footballroos' then?"

Very simple, mate. The Socceroos are a brand and you don't change the names of brands.

"But don't you think that for most people in Sydney going to the football means going to the rugby league?"

Probably. But other organisations do not run into problems referring to 'soccer' as football. Anyway, newspapers are doing it tough at the moment. In this present economic climate is it wise for News Limited to alienate itself from many football followers by its perceived biased coverage of the game?

"Look, for a start I do not work for a newspaper. I work for a news organisation which is equally internet and newspapers. We are the fastest-growing sports website in the country. In sport we break more stories on our website than any other organisation. Yes, newspapers are struggling a little bit but we do not deliberately try to upset soccer fans. We just do our best to provide a level coverage of the game. When Sydney FC and Newcastle won the league title we celebrated their success with them and we are strongly behind Central Coast, too. Yet all the football people do is hammer us for the negative stories we write. We are entitled to run those stories. I could just do without some of the death threats from the lunatics."

But you cannot refute the perception that News Limited is anti-football. You guys have an image problem.

"We probably do have a problem with our image among soccer fans. But how can we not highlight the unattractive brand of football the Socceroos are playing, for example."

So can we expect a decent coverage of the World Cup next year?

"Our coverage will be bigger and better than last time. Obviously the space we will throw at it will be determined by advertising support. Nobody supported the A-League when it started as we did. We had an eight-page liftout and had the full backing of the FFA. The *Sydney Morning Herald* throws a lot of space at rugby union because they get a lot of money from rugby advertising, we give rugby league plenty of space because we get a lot of money from rugby league advertising. If we get the same level of support during the World Cup we'll do the same with soccer. It's a magnificent event, probably equal to the Olympic Games. We'll do special editions and our website will update stories 24/7."

* * *

The financial problems that put Newcastle Jets on life support two years after they won the A-League were a huge concern for their supporters, not least local hero Craig Johnston.

Jets must not be allowed to die, pleads Johnston
18 September 2010

Craig Johnston, Newcastle's finest ever footballer, has made an impassioned plea to the city's fans to throw their full support behind the embattled Jets.

Newcastle, who won the A-League championship in 2008, have fallen on hard times and are on life support from Football Federation Australia as the club fights a desperate battle for survival.

The Jets' desperate plight has not gone unnoticed by Johnston, who was raised in the Hunter region before he went on to forge a brilliant career with Liverpool in the 1980s.

"Fans in Newcastle have to understand the importance of football in their city," Johnston, 50, said from Florida.

"You only need to recall that glorious day in 2008 when the Jets won the A-League to realise what football means to the place. We were all so proud.

"It was a glorious and uplifting period in the history of Newcastle football and today's fans have to protect the club's past by making sure it will live on."

Johnston said he was glad to hear that the Jets won their first league match of the season on Friday night when they beat Perth Glory 2–0 because he still considered himself a true-blue Novocastrian even though he has been away for so many years.

"You can take the boy out of Newcastle but you cannot take Newcastle out of the boy," he said.

"I always go to Lake Macquarie and to Nobbys Beach to watch the surf whenever I come home.

"I cannot follow the Jets as frequently as I would like to since I live in the USA and I travel a fair bit.

"But I was told a few months ago that the club was struggling and I was a bit concerned.

"I would like to help the club as best as I could and I hope that this story would touch the hearts of a few people.

"Some fans, you see, might not understand how vital Newcastle is to Australian football and vice versa and what rich heritage the whole region enjoys.

"So I urge the fans in the city to get out there and support the club in this hour of need."

Johnston said it was unthinkable that a club like Newcastle could be forced to fold when it enjoys such a wonderful sporting and cultural heritage.

"The club has profound Geordie links thanks to the English miners who came here at the turn of the century and helped start up a football club," Johnston explained.

"Football clubs in Newcastle are among the oldest in Australia, some even older than a few English Premier League clubs.

"The very name of the city plus those of such suburbs as Stockton and Gateshead are proof of Newcastle's strong links with the English city in the north-east.

"For people in the Hunter coal mining and football are everything.

"How can we let this heritage die?"

* * *

Hard man Kevin Muscat incurred the wrath of the A-League's followers with an X-rated tackle in the Melbourne derby in 2010-11.

Open letter to Kevin Muscat
23 January 2011

Kevin Muscat's disgraceful tackle on Melbourne City's Adrian Zahra at the weekend should be the signal for the Melbourne Victory veteran to call it a day.

This is an open letter to one of the hardest men in Australian football.

Dear Kevin,

If I know you as well as I think, you would be hurting badly from the barrage of criticism over your latest indiscretion on the field.

Your despicable tackle on young Adrian Zahra at the weekend brought howls of protest from anyone who has the true interest of the game at heart.

What the hell were you thinking?

For goodness' sake, you had just come back from suspension!

Kevin, I know you have apologised but I really wish you seriously consider calling it a day because you are doing your reputation, your club and your sport no favours with such unacceptable behaviour.

You have been one hell of a player and a true character of our game but if you do not recognise that Father Time has caught up with you big time, you are running the serious risk of being remembered for all the wrong reasons.

Mate, you are now 37, you have made your money and you will live comfortably for the rest of your life.

So why compromise your standing in the football fraternity by prolonging your career? You have nothing to prove to yourself or to anyone.

The readers' comments on the weekend derby on this website do not make for pleasant reading.

It's not particularly edifying to be called an embarrassment, a disgrace or even a thug ... and you should have seen the comments that were discarded by the moderator!

I can perfectly understand why you might have chosen not to let a penalty miss in last year's grand final be your last kick as a professional footballer.

However, put it this way: it would have been a much better way of going out than by maiming some player and getting banned for life.

I believe this has been a season too far for you and you have fallen into the common trap of not knowing when it's time to go.

You are still a born leader who exerts immense influence over your team.

And there would not be too many players in the A-League who could pass the ball as accurately and as positively as you do.

Your coach Ernie Merrick totally agreed with my suggestion after last week's match against Sydney FC that one realises how important you are to your team when you do not play.

But I'm sure you would agree that you have lost a bit of pace in the last couple of years and you are getting caught out more frequently by sprightly forwards who were born not long before you became a professional.

The timing of your tackles also is a bit off and this might make some challenges look worse than they actually are, as might have been the case at the weekend.

Kev, all through your career at home and abroad, you have pushed the boundaries of correctness and got away with it many times.

But you will have noticed that A-League referees are no longer prepared to give you the benefit of the doubt or be intimidated by your larger-than-life presence.

Which might just be another reason for you to look in the mirror and ask yourself: "Do I need this anymore?"

You might want to consider pulling the plug, putting your feet up and enjoying the personal rewards and satisfactions of a successful career.

You've done your bit in the trenches and you deserve a break.

Cheers, Philip

* * *

The 2011 grand final between Brisbane Roar and Central Coast Mariners was the best advertisement for the A-League. It was a privilege to be at the Suncorp spectacle.

Brisbane take out a grand final for the ages
13 March 2011

March 13, 2011, will go down as the day the A-League came of age and showed the rest of the country what a bloody fantastic competition we football people have.

If this superlative grand final between Brisbane Roar and Central Coast Mariners does not sell the game to mainstream Australia, nothing else will.

At the end of a physically draining, emotionally charged and spectacularly dramatic match that kept a 50,000 crowd on tenterhooks for 120 pulsating minutes, we had the added spectacle of a penalty shootout that brought this extraordinary contest to a fitting climax.

The Suncorp crowd heaved and throbbed and roared in support of the Brisbane side as they sought to add the championship to the premiership they had won with a few rounds to spare.

And when Brisbane achieved their cherished dream of a famous double, Suncorp erupted in a sea of unbridled passion and bedlam.

The Brisbane players could not contain their joy.

Some players wandered aimlessly trying to understand how they could be celebrating a victory that had seemed highly unlikely only minutes earlier.

Some went over to one end of the stadium to salute their fans.

Others just collapsed on the ground under the weight of the raw emotion while Henrique was in tears not long after slotting home the winning penalty and had to be comforted.

One felt really sorry for Graham Arnold and his brave Mariners who, let's face it, were slightly the better team and could have won. Make that, should have won.

But football being football and Brisbane being Brisbane, one just knew that even when Roar were two goals down with four minutes to go, all they needed was a sniff of a chance and they certainly would take it, as they have done so many times this season.

And, boy, didn't they take it!

The Mariners were on their way to their first championship after losing two grand finals when Adam Kwasnik and Oliver Bozanic carved out the Roar defence to give their side a two-goal lead in the first period of extra time.

But when little man Henrique pulled a goal back three minutes from time, Roar knew they had a chance.

And so did the crowd which sensed something special was about to unfold.

With virtually seconds left till the final whistle and most of the 50,000 fans willing them on, Thomas Broich took an inswinging corner that was met by the powerful frame of big man Erik Paartalu who stabbed the ball home with a bullet header.

The roar that greeted the last-gasp goal was deafening and nearly lifted the roof of Suncorp.

"I had given up hope when the Mariners were two goals up," Brisbane hero Paartalu said later.

"I thought this was not going to be our day but a rousing talk from captain Matt McKay between the two periods of extra time brought the belief back in our team.

"He told us 'we have scored twice in 15 minutes before so let's do it again' and we responded.

"The way we finished summed up our season, really."

Football is alive and well in Australia.

*   *   *

Graham Arnold's coaching reputation soared to new heights after he led Central Coast Mariners to the 2012 A-League premiership.

The reincarnation of Graham Arnold
29 March 2012

Graham Arnold has defied the odds with his premiership-winning Central Coast Mariners and shattered a few myths about his coaching ability along the way.

Arnold's image as an aspiring coach was at a low ebb four years ago as he sought to make a mark on the managerial side of football.

As coach of Australia's Olyroos, the former striker who played 54 times for his country was roundly criticised after the team's early exit from the football tournament of the Beijing Olympics.

He also was in charge of the national team during their unspectacular AFC Asian Cup campaign in 2007 when they lost to Japan on penalties in the quarter-finals.

His brief appointment as interim Socceroos coach came between stints as assistant to World Cup coaches Guus Hiddink in 2006 and Pim Verbeek in 2010.

The general feeling among many Australian pundits was that he was an able lieutenant but he lacked the qualities and experience to be a commander.

Fast forward to 2012 and Arnold is basking in the glory of a far more respectful stature after adapting himself effortlessly to the day-to-day routine of club coaching.

Arnold's star continued to rise at the weekend when his Mariners side secured the A-League premiership in his second season as club coach.

This week he was rewarded for his efforts by being named A-League coach of the year by Professional Footballers Australia, the players' union.

This success arrived a year after the Mariners came within seconds of beating Brisbane Roar in an epic grand final that will be remembered for a long time.

Arnold, described by *The Australian* this week as "more blue singlet than white collar", has done all this without any big names other teams could count on.

Rival coaches had the luxury of dealing with such crowd-pullers as Thomas Broich, Besart Berisha, Paul Ifill, Shane Smeltz, Brett Emerton, Nick Carle, Harry Kewell, Archie Thompson and Fred.

However Arnold had to make do with a blend of experienced players and emerging youths that has yielded a hard-working and dependable outfit that thrives on an uncompromising defence and a crafty midfield.

Never has the adage that a champion team is better than a team of champions rung truer.

The Mariners are a more refined outfit these days after shedding the 'no frills' tag that was unkindly bestowed upon them since day one, probably because they were always seen as a battling team that punched above their weight.

The fluent passing game developed by Arnold is beginning to pay dividends because the Mariners seem to be the only team in Australia with the capacity to consistently trouble Ange Postecoglou's Roar.

Brisbane's 5–1 bashing in Gosford 16 months ago seems like a distant memory now.

And Arnold, 48, could only achieve this by keeping his players focused in the good times and during a period of turbulence in the latter part of this season that could have aborted the Mariners' flight to glory.

He has strengthened the camaraderie in the dressing room that was the hallmark of his predecessor Lawrie McKinna and kept his players' feet well and truly on the ground.

Which is not an easy task considering the widespread media attention given to whiz kids Matthew Ryan, Mustafa Amini, Bernie Ibini and more recently Tomas Rogic.

A few weeks ago, when the Mariners were leading the competition by a commanding 11 points, I rang Arnold to ask him if he would be tempted to rotate his squad in the last rounds of the league so as to fit in the club's tough AFC Champions League commitments.

"Speak to me when we secure the title, we're not there yet," Arnold told me bluntly.

Arnold's point was that football is a strange and unpredictable game and has a way of making people look silly for making hasty statements.

Arnold's concern was vindicated almost immediately because the team suffered a form slump with the finish line in sight and they only secured their richly deserved premiership in the last round of the competition proper, beating Wellington Phoenix 2-1 away.

It is a measure of the self-belief that Arnold has instilled in his players that they overcame a difficult period in the face of hot Brisbane pressure by going back to the basics and grinding out results.

What the 2012 Premiers' Plate means is that the Mariners will be playing in next year's Champions League, giving the cash-strapped club another opportunity to raise its profile and boost its brand in Asia.

The Mariners have secured two draws in their opening matches against China's Tianjin Teda and Japan's Nagoya Grampus in this year's tournament and would have an excellent chance of reaching the knockout phase if they beat Korea Republic's Seongnam Ilhwa at Bluetongue Stadium next Tuesday.

A more immediate benefit of winning the premiership is that the Mariners will go into the finals series as favourites to win the title that has eluded them since the league started in 2005-06.

The Mariners face Brisbane at Suncorp on Friday in the first leg of the major semi-final.

They feel quite at home at Suncorp and they won 2-1 the last time they played there.

And the Mariners' belief in their ability to go toe to toe with Brisbane is such that Arnold would be entitled to feel quietly confident about the outcome of the match.

And this is all due to the work behind the scenes that has made his former critics eat their words.

Graham Arnold may or may not lead the Mariners to their first championship but he has certainly come a long way as a football coach.

* * *

The A-League's first Sydney derby in 2012 at a buzzing Parramatta Stadium met all expectations. I watched history being made.

Sydney derby's power and the passion
21 October 2012

It's been a long time coming but in the end we got there and Sydney has a derby to be proud of.

The hyped-up confrontation between Western Sydney Wanderers and Sydney FC lived up to all expectations and every person lucky enough to be at a heaving Parramatta Stadium would have left the venue yearning for more.

It was a football festival of colour, noise, passion and drama that must have come across as a powerful spectacle on television as well.

The Sydney derby was as big a smash hit with the fans as its Melbourne equivalent was two seasons ago.

The match vindicated the Wanderers' decision to stick with Parramatta Stadium even for their big games.

The 19,126 crowd that crammed into the stadium to create a European-style spectacle would have been lost in a bigger venue like ANZ Stadium even though the attendance would have been larger.

From a technical perspective Wanderers and Sydney are still a work in progress and, putting it bluntly, on the evidence of the first three rounds of the competition they are not likely to win the A-League championship.

Yet derbies are not beauty contests. They are special events where full commitment and esprit de corps are what fans pay to see and demand.

And credit to both sets of players who threw everything at each other in a valiant attempt to gain supremacy on such a historic occasion.

A close-range finish from Italian superstar Alessandro Del Piero after his retaken penalty had been parried gave Sydney a 1–0 victory, their first of the season.

Yet many neutrals—not that there were many at the stadium—probably would have felt sorry for the Wanderers as they continue their quest for a maiden win and first goal of the season.

Coach Tony Popovic is building a solid side that is more than capable of playing out from the back and enjoy a fair share of possession.

However, he needs more bite in attack.

What would he give for a Del Piero, an Emile Heskey or even a Shane Smeltz, Besart Berisha or Archie Thompson!

As so often happens, a tight derby with no quarter asked or given can be decided by a flash of pure class.

That moment came nine minutes into the second half when Del Piero won possession of the ball, waltzed his way into a crowded penalty area and expertly drew a foul from young Aaron Mooy, who otherwise played another good game in the heart of the midfield for the Wanderers.

Del Piero found the net at the third time of asking.

He scored with his first kick but the penalty had to be retaken due to encroachment.

His second kick was saved by Ante Covic but he showed poise and alertness to slam the ball home from the rebound to send the hundreds of Sydney fans into raptures.

To their immense credit the Wanderers supporters kept urging on their heroes until the very end but forwards Dino Kresinger and Mark Bridge failed to reward the fans' passion with a goal that would not have been undeserved.

There was not much in it but Sydney perhaps legitimised their victory by the way they controlled their lead.

Popovic spoke later about "goals that change games" while Ian Crook hailed his players for their better use of the ball than in the first two matches.

Sydney have a long way to go to be considered genuine challengers for the title.

It would appear that they do not enjoy the organisation of Brisbane Roar, the effervescence of Melbourne Victory or the toughness of Central Coast Mariners.

Yet with Del Piero beginning to adjust to life in the A-League, Brett Emerton running into form and Pascal Bosschaart getting closer to a return from injury, who knows what's in store for the Sky Blues.

In the meantime, fans of both teams are already counting the days to the next derby at Allianz Stadium on 15 December.

Bring it on.

* * *

'QUOTE UNQUOTE'

A xenophobic and tasteless cartoon in a big-selling daily newspaper raised serious concerns as Australia prepared to stage the 2015 Asian Cup.

Media bigotry rears its ugly head again
27 January 2014

The Australian media's understanding of multiculturalism and football's place in Asia has come under the microscope.

This time next year Australian football fans should be in seventh heaven and rubbing their hands in anticipation as the AFC Asian Cup reaches its climax with the final in Sydney.

Hopefully Australia will get the chance to avenge its painful 1–0 defeat against Japan in the final of the last Asian Cup in Qatar in 2011.

The 16-team competition is being hailed as the biggest sporting event to be held in Australia since the 2000 Olympic Games.

A successful tournament from the home team would go a long way towards making it a raging success.

It is also very important for Australia to be able to put on a show for our Asian guests and let them know that it very much sees itself as part of the continent's massive football family. Easier said than done.

There should be no problem with the organisation of the tournament: Australia has a proven record for holding first-class events.

Events of the past week, however, have made it very clear that we still have a big job on our hands to convince our Asian friends that we have shed the perceived image of a bunch of rampant rednecks who look down on Asia with a superiority complex that is both unjustified and embarrassing.

Melbourne's *Herald Sun*, Australia's biggest-selling daily newspaper, published a cringeworthy cartoon the day after Abu Dhabi-backed Manchester City bought a majority share in A-League club Melbourne Heart.

The sensational takeover was a positive story whichever way you look at it.

Yet the notorious daily that is so sensitive to unsocial behaviour from football fans thought nothing of the damage xenophobia can cause to the tepid relations between Australia and some of our Asian neighbours at diplomatic level.

In a case of bad taste at best and blatant racism at worst, it published a cartoon depicting an Arab sheikh and a set of 'cheer girls' dressed in black burqas ushering the Heart team onto the field.

A caption read "That should sheikh up the A-League".

What on earth was the *Herald Sun* thinking?

Did it think at all about the ramifications of publishing such a tasteless cartoon in the present political climate?

Did it realise that as host country of the 2015 Asian Cup it is Australia's obligation to welcome the participants, not poke fun at their culture?

Did it really believe that its hundreds of thousands of readers would approve of such ignorance and opportunism or, more seriously, find it funny?

Did it honestly expect to get away with its flagrant disregard for basic human courtesy?

Australia arguably embraces multiculturalism like no other country and the *Herald Sun's* cartoon went against everything that we stand for.

I refuse to believe that there were more sinister motives at play here like purposely damaging the event's credibility behind the publication of the controversial cartoon.

However, if the newspaper's intention was merely to have some fun, surely it must have known that what is considered 'just a bit of fun' by us might not be seen as 'fun' by people from a different background, whether they live in Australia, Indonesia or Iran.

If, as I suspect, the paper smugly regards the negative reaction to the cartoon as vindication for publishing it in the first place it should hang its head in shame.

The *Herald Sun*, to be fair, is not the first publication or medium to show a level of ignorance about such delicate matters and it won't be the last.

The media, after all, by and large reflects the attitude and mentality of the people it is supposed to serve.

Which is why the football family as one must distance itself in no uncertain terms from such xenophobia.

Many would argue that free speech is one of the cornerstones of what it means to be Australian and it is certainly not the intention of this columnist to dispute the right of any media organisation to publish or transmit any material it likes as long as it is legal.

Yet since we live in a free country we also reserve the right to deplore such examples of crassness in no uncertain terms.

In a football country that is hell-bent on leaving a strong and lasting impression on billions of Asians, it is important that every effort be made to look after the interests of the game.

The Asian Cup will provide Australia with a unique opportunity to forge stronger cultural and economic links with Asia and give football yet another fillip.

Which is why the game should fight for its rights.

And if it can't stop its 'enemies' from causing their own brand of collateral damage, the least it should do is stand up for itself and let the whole country know that it is being treated unfairly.

It is well worth reminding ourselves that average Australians are smart enough to know what's right and what's wrong.

The anti-football mafia's game will be up one day.

You see, you can fool some people some of the time but you can't fool all the people all the time.

Those in the media who are hell-bent on painting football in a bad light should take note.

* * *

The creation of the FFA Cup knockout competition filled a much-needed void in Australia's football calendar.

The magic of cup football comes to Australia
29 July 2014

Australian club football will enter an exciting era when the keenly anticipated FFA Cup kicks off in four suburban grounds this week.

'Old soccer' finally gets an opportunity to mix it with the 'new football' in a national knockout that could become a permanent fixture in Australia's sporting landscape if everything goes according to plan.

Twenty-two teams from every state and territory, among them some clubs that played a key role in the establishment of our game, have emerged from a long qualifying phase to join the A-League's 10 clubs in the competition proper.

Most football fans from across Australia are intrigued by the cup concept and would be expecting the competition to be a knockout in more ways than one.

The tiny and unassuming Wanderers Oval in Broadmeadow (NNSW), Kingston Heath Soccer Complex in Cheltenham (Victoria), Cromer Park in Dee Why (NSW) and Goodwin Park in Yeronga (Queensland) will create history when they simultaneously host the first four matches of the round of 32.

The remaining 12 ties will be played over the next three weeks.

The game in Australia has been crying out for a cup competition to supplement the A-League for a number of years.

As the league kept taking small but strong steps forward, the sentimentalists among us have yearned for a knockout tournament that could provide the occasional dose of romance and magic.

Now that it is a reality, the FFA Cup should appease the Asian Football Confederation which requires every top country to stage an annual knockout competition.

The FFA Cup will also give the modern game a chance to acknowledge its past in a spirit of camaraderie.

There are still many who rightly or wrongly have not forgotten the so-called 'ethnic cleansing' of the game to make way for the A-League.

The game's rebirth in 2005 has created more than a technical and organisational disparity between the elite A-League and its semi-professional and amateur counterparts.

Hopefully the cup will bridge that gap and bring both parties closer together for the good of our game.

Which is why it was disappointing to learn of Perth Glory's pull-out from a pre-season match with Sydney Olympic at Belmore last week.

Glory claimed their players had no opportunity to adequately prepare for the match and stormed off the ground two hours before kick-off.

Glory may have had their reasons to pull out of the game yet the timing of the incident, which came days before the FFA Cup kick-off, was unfortunate.

The club admitted that the walk-out was a setback in its preparation for the forthcoming A-League, where competition is expected to be as tough and uncompromising as ever.

While the salary cap has created an equilibrium in the league, the cup is expected to thrive on its inequalities and disparities.

Everybody dreams of a giant-killing act from one of the National Premier Leagues clubs at the expense of their professional opponents.

Shock results are the fabric of such competitions, none more so than in England, Germany, Spain and France where the FA Cup, DFB-Pokal, Copa del Rey and Coupe de France are treated with the utmost respect by the fans if not by some of the biggest clubs which have higher priorities.

When Broadmeadow Magic take on Brisbane Strikers, South Springvale face South Cardiff, Manly United lock horns with Sydney Olympic and Olympic FC challenge Melbourne Knights on Tuesday night, players and fans of the eight teams involved no doubt will have justifiable dreams of glory right from the very first whistle.

There have been several attempts to create a knockout tournament over the last 35 years or so but the concept never caught the imagination of a sceptical public.

It is too early to tell if the cup's modern version will succeed where several others have failed.

Certainly the midweek evening fixtures will test the fans' resolve.

With the full backing of FFA, Westfield, television and the media, augmented by a prevailing air of genuine goodwill, our game will never get a better chance of cherishing a respected knockout competition.

FFA will foot the bill for the away teams' travel expenses while the home teams will meet the costs of holding the matches but they will get to keep the gate money.

So everything is in place for the competition's grand entry.

Of course, the bottom line is that nothing will stir the fans' emotions more than a shock result involving an A-League club but it does not necessarily have to be so.

The fact that little known Stirling Lions from suburban Perth will get an opportunity to entertain A-League champions Brisbane Roar and former National Soccer League champions South Coast Wolves will be back in the national limelight when they host 2013 A-League champions Central Coast Mariners is enough to whet the appetite of even the most discerning fans.

The event has been formatted in such a way that there will be a presence from outside the A-League in the latter stages of the competition that reaches its climax with the cup final on 16 December.

A totally open draw would have been great but the piloted exercise is understandable in the present circumstances, given the competition is still in its infancy.

So let's all enjoy this flight of fancy and see where it takes us.

* * *

Western Sydney Wanderers caused a major sensation by winning the 2014 AFC Champions League only three years after the club's creation.

Australian football should follow Wanderers' lead
3 November 2014

The extraordinary achievement of Western Sydney Wanderers to become champions of Asia less than three years after they were born out of the Gold Coast United fracas should be the seminal moment in Australian club football.

Not necessarily because the Wanderers' incredible feat will put the A-League on the world map and boost the general confidence in the competition.

The aggregate defeat of Saudi Arabia's Al Hilal should serve as a clarion call to other clubs that are older than the Wanderers to lift their collective game when it comes to taking on Asia's finest in the AFC Champions League.

The Socceroos, too, should see the Wanderers' win as the tonic they need to have a real crack at the AFC Asian Cup on home soil in January.

The Wanderers rode their luck in Riyadh and survived three strong penalty appeals to snare the title against all the odds with a defensive style of play that is unlikely to endear Australian football to the rest of the continent.

Make no mistake, Al Hilal played the better football over the two legs even though their finishing never matched their eye-catching approach.

It would be churlish, however, to dwell on these negatives after an overwhelmingly positive night for the club and Australian football.

Adelaide United's ascent to the 2008 final pales into insignificance now when compared with the Wanderers' triumph that will be talked about for a long time.

The million-dollar question that now needs to be put to the A-League is this: if the three year-old Wanderers club could find a top coach, build a strong team that is supported by thousands of members and go on to win the biggest prize in Asian football, why cannot establishment clubs such as Melbourne Victory, Brisbane Roar, Sydney FC and Adelaide do the same thing?

If Popovic can leave his mark on the Asian game by playing to his players' strengths and opposition's weaknesses, why cannot Ange Postecoglou do the same at national level in three months?

The 'nowhere men' from Parramatta proved that it can be done.

This is the challenge the Wanderers have set the rest of Australia as they savour an Arabian night and look ahead to the FIFA Club World Cup in Morocco in December, where they face Cruz Azul of Mexico in the quarter-finals.

Adelaide's run to the final six years ago was seen as a one-off that was unlikely to be repeated, especially since China has now become a big player in the competition.

A-League clubs have suffered several debilitating defeats at the hands of J.League and K League Classic mega sides since 2008.

The Wanderers, in their first sortie into Asia, have shown what rewards await salary-capped Australian clubs if they do things the right way, recruit wisely and play to their strengths.

When Popovic was unveiled as coach of the yet unnamed entity in May 2012, I asked him what it felt like to be manager of a club with no players.

"I certainly did not envisage this but this is the exciting part of it, the challenge," he said.

"We have a blank piece of paper and piece by piece we need to fill that paper up in all areas of the club.

"We know we'll get there, we'll have our bumps along the way but we have a clear goal and vision for the club.

"I have actually no doubt that it will be a success. That's why I've taken up the challenge."

He would meet that challenge with a dedication and bloody-mindedness that surprised even those who know him well.

The four A-League clubs with the largest supporter bases and the deepest pockets will no doubt publicly express their delight at the Western Sydney club's feats that will benefit them in the long run because the A-League brand has been enhanced by its resurgence in Riyadh.

Privately they should see this as a wake-up call and they should ask themselves: "If the Wanderers can do it, why can't we?"

Postecoglou might prefer his players to seek glory in a different way but no doubt he will have been impressed with the firm resolve and refusal to be beaten shown by Popa's men.

The Wanderers no doubt have done Australian football proud.

Yet if their achievement gives other A-League clubs and the Socceroos the confidence to lift their game against the cream of Asia they will have given football in this country an even more significant boost.

* * *

Milos Ninkovic's masterful displays for Sydney FC showed that the A-League was better off with quality foreigners in their prime than costly superstars who were well past their peak.

Why a Ninkovic is always better than a Del Piero
9 October 2017

Sydney FC playmaker Milos Ninkovic consolidated his reputation as one of the finest and most influential imports in the history of the A-League by delivering yet another master class at the weekend.

The slick Serb played a major part in the Sky Blues' championship and premiership double last season and he left no doubt about his drive and ambition to do it all over again by stealing the show in the Big Blue against Melbourne Victory which Sydney won 1–0.

The statistics will show that the match was decided by an own goal from Thomas Deng.

What they will not reveal is the top-class performance from Sydney's master of ceremonies who added glamour to the big occasion with several prime examples of his jaw-dropping skill and flair.

Ninkovic was here, there and everywhere and even found time to play a number of incredible passes that took your breath away. He rightly was named man of the match.

In the second half he found David Carney with a through ball of such surgical precision, from a difficult position in his own half, that the substitute striker must have been surprised that the vertical pass actually came off.

On another occasion Ninkovic was standing on the edge of the 'D' and he nonchalantly flicked the ball backwards to free up Luke Wilkshire but the overlapping fullback saw his shot across goal saved by Lawrence Thomas.

There was talk towards the end of last season that Ninkovic, who played for Serbia against Australia at the 2010 FIFA World Cup, might not extend his two-year contract.

But Sydney wisely tempted Ninkovic with marquee status and he put pen on paper on a new deal only days after slotting home the winning penalty in the grand final shootout against Victory in May.

"Not only is he a great player but he is a great 'team' man," coach Graham Arnold says of his star.

"His work rate is fantastic. He is a dream to coach."

Ninkovic's success in Sydney is a compelling argument for those who maintain that the A-League is better off looking for reliable imports of a sufficiently high standard than by being blinded by expensive big names that are at the end of their careers.

It is all well and good for the A-League to draw such genuine superstars as Alessandro Del Piero who was the kind of guy to put bums on seats wherever he played.

Yet Sydney themselves would probably admit that the Italian legend was not such an overwhelming success on the field of play in his second season when he clearly showed his age. He was 39 when he left Sydney.

Del Piero scored some memorable goals in his first season but he was unable to make the difference to a Sky Blues side that admittedly was much poorer individually and collectively than it is now.

Ninkovic, on the other hand, has been consistently strong since he came here in 2015 at a fraction of Del Piero's cost and I have no qualms about declaring that his overall contribution to the Sky Blues' cause is more telling than that of the more famous 'Pinturicchio'.

Ninkovic is not the only quality foreigner to light up the league despite lacking a superstar billing.

Crowd-pulling attackers such as Carlos Hernandez, Gui Finkler, Thomas Broich,

Besart Berisha, Marcos Flores, Diego Castro, Marcelo Carrusca and Bruno Fornaroli came to Australia as virtual unknowns but they have left an indelible mark on the competition with their very special deeds on the field. Some of the goals they scored will be remembered for many years.

Sydney's major signing Adrian Mierzejewski is already looking the part and the Polish international could become just as successful and influential.

The same can be said of Western Sydney Wanderers' new Spanish signings Oriol Riera, Alvaro Cejudo and Raul Llorente.

Sydney are not the only club that appears to understand the value of a classy foreigner who is not necessarily a major international star.

Sure, Del Piero and Dwight Yorke before him were engaged mainly as a means of raising the club's profile and boosting home gates.

But the overwhelming success of consistent Ninkovic illustrates very clearly that if any individual plays a key part in improving his team then the long-term playing and economic benefits would outweigh the Band-Aid solution the acquisition of a big-name has-been can provide.

* * *

World Cup defender Craig Moore called for the FFA to relinquish control of club football as the A-League continued its downward spiral.

A-League clubs must break away, says Moore
2 November 2017

Socceroos legend Craig Moore has called for Football Federation Australia to relinquish control of the A-League as boardroom brawls continue to overshadow the game.

Moore, who played for Australia at the 2006 and 2010 FIFA World Cups, said he was deeply dismayed by the poor governance that is damaging the game.

He feels football's administrators are letting down the coaches and players who collectively have lifted their game this season, saying the only solution is for the FFA to continue to govern the national teams and let the A-League be run independently.

"You've got to have a breakaway because too many people have no confidence in the FFA which tells you that change has to happen sooner rather than later," Moore said.

"Australian football is in a very delicate situation. We are at the crossroads.

"The natural progression for our game is for FFA to administer the national teams and an independent body to look after the league.

"FFA should make sure that the national teams and their programs are fully resourced and the players (are) given the best chance to fulfil their potential.

"The A-League clubs and those in the second and third tiers need an opportunity to grow the game because they are not getting it at the moment."

Moore, who is now director of football at Brisbane Roar, is deeply concerned by football's inability to build on the initial success of the A-League and the achievements of the so-called 'Golden Generation' of which he formed a major part.

He feels the current business model in which the FFA pockets the profits from the A-League finals series, while placing restrictions on the sponsors clubs can sign, only serves to hamstring the league's growth.

"The ongoing saga about the congress is a clear indication that there is unrest," Moore said.

"A lot of people are very unhappy with the direction the game in Australia is taking with FFA in control.

"You have 10 A-League clubs that have come together to fight for change. There is no opportunity as things stand for clubs to prosper.

"There are a lot of restrictions to the business model. Clubs don't benefit from the finals which are the biggest games of the season that draw the biggest gates, they don't gain enough from the sale of merchandise and they have some real issues in bringing new sponsors to the table such as car manufacturers.

"FFA are clearly under-resourced and when huge important cuts are made like closing the Centre of Excellence and cancelling a tour abroad for the Under-23s, one is entitled to feel a lack of confidence in the leaders of our game.

"There is a lot of anger within the media while those at the coalface feel a great frustration because we all want to take this game forward."

* * *

Adamstown Rosebud, one of Australia's oldest football clubs, have produced three Socceroos during their 130-year history.

How a 130-year-old club survives despite all odds
25 June 2019

They have survived two world wars, an economic depression, a killer earthquake, relegation and the emergence of Newcastle Knights and Newcastle Jets yet Adamstown Rosebud Football Club are still swinging and punching above their weight.

Adamstown, who play in the Northern NSW division of the National Premier Leagues, are one of Australia's oldest surviving clubs.

At the weekend they celebrated their 130th anniversary with a gala night at the Wests New Lambton leagues club in Newcastle, about half an hour's walk from their traditional home ground Adamstown Oval.

It was at that modest venue which was then surrounded by bushland that the Adamstown club was formed on a cold Friday night on 12 July 1889, a whole decade before Italian giants AC Milan were formed.

A month later 'Rosebud' beat such options as Wanderers, Rangers, Thistle and Pirates as the preferred additional name and the team's colours of blue and white were established.

Rosebud would later change their colours to the current red and green.

Adamstown Rosebud are to Newcastle football what South Coast United were to Wollongong.

They are synonymous with football in the Hunter even though their only major trophy came in 1984 when as a reincarnation of National Soccer League club Newcastle KB United that had gone bankrupt, they won the NSL Cup by beating Melbourne Croatia 1–0 in the final at Olympic Park.

They also won the regional premiership 11 times and the grand final on five occasions in the club's golden period from 1961 to 1991.

Adamstown's greatest contribution to the game in Australia, however, was providing a platform from which three Newcastle-born players made a name for themselves as fully fledged and much loved Socceroos.

Defender Col Curran played in Australia's three matches at the 1974 FIFA World Cup and striker Ray Baartz would have joined him had he not suffered a brutal foul in a pre-tournament friendly with Uruguay that ended his career prematurely.

Both played first grade for Adamstown in the 1960s before moving on to greener pastures.

Fullback Graham Jennings was another Socceroos star who came through the club ranks.

He played his junior football for Rosebud before being snapped up by Sydney Olympic in 1979.

Midfielder Joe Senkalski, who would achieve great success in the National Soccer League with Sydney Olympic and Newcastle, was also a Rosebud product.

Baartz said he was privileged to have played a part in Rosebud's colourful history.

"As a kid I was down at the oval all the time and all I wanted to do was play for my local team," he told a 250-strong gathering in Newcastle comprising a who's who of the Hunter's football community.

"You always played outside the oval and you dreamed of getting inside the oval and playing.

"There was a wooden fence surrounding the pitch those days and since we did not have money to pay to get in we used to climb the fence to watch the games so when I donned the red and green jersey for the first time it meant everything to me.

"In the 1950s and early 1960s Adamstown were the team, not just in Newcastle but in Australia."

Rosebud president John Connors said the club that is steeped in history and tradition has survived for all these years amid considerable drawbacks due to the sterling work of volunteers but he revealed he hoped that the club would become more competitive on the field.

"The club always finds ways to fight back and it's mainly the spirit of our volunteers that sees us through all the time," Connors said.

"Having said that, we would love to become a regular mid-table team instead of one that is often floundering near the bottom of the league.

"It would also be nice to get to the round of 32 of the FFA Cup and join our big brothers the Jets."

The atmosphere at the anniversary function was one of celebration of the club's longevity and pride in its contribution to the game in Australia.

The prevailing mood also provided a poignant reminder that although the professional game in Australia is beset with problems and unsure of its long-term future, a little club like Adamstown Rosebud that is held together by volunteers who have their club and the game at heart has shown that nothing is impossible when there is a strong and united will to survive.

* * *

Flamboyant Italian midfielder Alessandro Diamanti said he rejected an offer to play in Serie A in order to play in Australia and captain the A-League's new club Western United.

Dazzling Diamanti snubbed Serie A for A-League
13 August 2020

Western United captain Alessandro Diamanti, the 'smiling assassin' who will be remembered as one of the A-League's finest imports, revealed he knocked back an offer to join a Serie A club because he could not refuse the new challenge of playing in Australia.

Diamanti, 37, joined the A-League's newest club in their first year last July and has led them to the finals with two matches to spare.

The Italy international, who featured in the 2012 European Championships, feels his success down under has justified his decision to snub one of Europe's major leagues in favour of the A-League.

"I was playing in the second division last year and I had a few offers to return to Serie A," Diamanti said.

"I was just about to sign for a Serie A club that was in the top half of the table when I got a call from Western United who explained to me their ambitious project that had me as the team's centrepiece.

"It was a fascinating prospect because, let's face it, another season in Serie A would not have changed my life. I would have made a few more bucks in Italy but at this stage of my career these things do not matter a great deal.

"I saw the opportunity as a new experience for myself and my family and we came here with an open mind.

"It was an easy decision—a no-brainer really—especially for a player of my age."

Western United's acquisition of Diamanti did not come easy.

Sources revealed no firm attempt was made by any A-League club to sign Diamanti before the Western organisation last year applied for financial assistance from Football Federation Australia via the special marquee fund.

Western's overtures were knocked back because the governing body did not deem the Italian maestro famous enough for marketing purposes.

The club had no other alternative but to go it alone.

Diamanti said he knew very little of what was going on behind the scenes but when asked if he was surprised by the governing body's stance he said simply: "They were right!"

"Anyway, I really cannot comment on this because I did not know the ins and outs of the case.

"To be honest, this did not concern me too much because I was close to coming here and I was able to sign for the club. This is life."

Diamanti was signed on a one-year deal but has since extended his contract for another two seasons.

* * *

Australian Professional Leagues boss Danny Townsend talked about the independent body's plans for the A-League.

Get behind us and we'll deliver, vows APL boss
10 June 2021

The Australian Professional Leagues has made an impassioned plea to all football lovers of this country to get behind the club game as it enters a new phase of its long and tortured road to sustainability.

The A-League and W-League, fresh from being unbundled from Football Australia, have been bolstered by a $200m deal with Channel 10 and Paramount+ that should usher in an era of prosperity from next season.

The APL has bold plans for its showpiece competitions but the independent body says every decision it makes will have the fans as front and centre.

The body also believes that league football should kick out the inferiority complex that has hindered the game's progress for decades.

"The game's stakeholders and governance over many years lost sight of the needs of the fans, the participants, the parents, the coaches, the managers, the members," managing director Danny Townsend said.

"In any business, you have to put your customer first. Unfortunately, our game did not make that decision.

"The APL is all about driving outcomes for the fans and provide a better experience for them. People need to engage with our game and this will ultimately move the football economy forward. It's about putting the fans at the centre of every decision we make. That's the key difference.

"We've always been a bit apologetic about Australian football and where our game sits in the broader sporting landscape. It's always been on the periphery. Okay, it's not the Premier League or as technical as La Liga but you know what ... it's our football and we should be really proud of it.

"We need to break into the centre of Australian sporting culture and celebrate the role football has played in the waves of migrants who came to this country. Old Australians, new Australians ... it does not matter who you are ... everyone has an affinity with the game and a story and experience to tell and we need to bring those to light. We need to give these people something that is uniquely Australian to hang on to.

"If we do that and think this way we will unlock a huge opportunity for our game."

Townsend, who doubles up as Sydney FC chief executive, also addressed the concerns of many league followers in this transitional phase of Australian club football.

The league has achieved its independence and is free to run its own show to a degree. How are the relations with Football Australia?

"Our relationship is fine and we have now settled into our respective areas of responsibility. We are really focused on doing what we need to do to make our areas as successful as can be. We are working collectively with the FA to get the outcome we all need for the football fans and participants. It's a relationship that has taken on a new paradigm but so far so good."

Can you give us some more details on the deal with Channel 10 and Paramount+?

"The main points of the deal are twofold. It gives us the reach which we have craved for a long time so the free-to-air audience which we will be able to achieve on a Saturday night will be first on a commercial network. And the launch of Paramount+ that will have football as the central pillar of its sports proposition is another important piece to the deal that made it really attractive."

Many fans fear a 'big bash league' approach to football coverage and ads during play. Should they be worried?

"What Ten did for the 'big bash' is unprecedented. They took a sport that was in decline and turned it into a juggernaut of the Australian sporting landscape. They intend to do the same with us.

"That doesn't mean that has to be done in a way that compromises the integrity of the broadcast or the 90 minutes that remain sacrosanct to our game. I think fans can take comfort from the fact that our conversations with Ten have been enormously respectful of our game. Equally, we have added that on top there are certain FIFA regulations in place to ensure that certain aspects of the game are sacrosanct.

"Ten are very aware of this and we are genuinely excited about the entertainment factor Ten will bring to the broadcast. Not just the broadcast itself but, more importantly, the noise around it through magazine-style programming and graphic profiles. I don't think fans should be concerned. They should be excited, to be honest."

The competition will be played primarily in the warmer months which goes against the FA's desire to align its seasons and play in winter. Do you expect a few problems with head office down the track?

"Not at all. I speak with (FA chief executive) James Johnson most days about several matters and obviously, the domestic match calendar is an issue that is critically important for everyone in the game, not just the A-League or W-League.

"Working collaboratively with the FA, James has been very clear to me: he is not against any type of seasonality around our game. He wants to ensure that the match calendar caters for everyone and we are working to make sure that that is the case.

We absolutely do not see any problems with that dynamic, moving forward."

Will the salary cap stay and if it does what is the figure likely to be?

"We are in talks with the PFA over the collective bargaining agreement. The cap and playing conditions are obviously being negotiated so I won't be talking publicly about the matter out of respect for the PFA. We are confident of, as always, finding a way forward with the PFA to do what's right for the game and ensure that the model we work towards is sustainable."

Football was hit hard by the pandemic with viewership and attendances declining. How will the new league win back those people?

"As I said, an important part of the APL strategy is to put the fans first. To do that, the fans need to understand when the games are on. The marketing of the game has let us down in recent years and our focus will be on making sure the A-League and W-League are talked about on as many different channels and platforms as we can. It's all about driving that awareness of what we will be doing on the football field. We know we have enormous strength in the number of participants and fans who love football.

"Our challenge is to convert those participants into A-League or W-League fans and to bring back those fans who have lapsed by giving them a reason to re-engage. It will be about serving them with great content that we know they'll love."

The standard of this A-League season has been one of the best in the competition's history yet there is a general apathy among stakeholders. Does this show very clearly how difficult it is for football to win the hearts and minds of average Australians?

"Absolutely, it's a challenge. We are competing with many entertainment platforms for our fans' time. And being able to do that effectively is going to be central to the re-imagining of our leagues. That's the first step. It's also about re-energising the football fans, getting them to believe again. We know they believe in football, we want them to believe in Australian football. And that is what the APL is all about. We are confident that if we engage our fans more effectively they will come back in droves and help football rise up the table and become the biggest sport in Australia in 2030. That's our goal."

Former FFA chief executive David Gallop said something similar during his time. Are we setting ourselves up for failure by making such bold declarations in a country that is besotted with Australian Rules football and rugby league?

"I don't think so. We need to be confident and have the conviction that our sport is number one in the world. How to make sure we are able to deliver that same experience in Australia? The reality is the A-League is a 16-year-old proposition. Yes, we had the NSL which was fantastic and before that we had organised football for quite some time.

"But in terms of a professional league we are only half a generation old and we need to ensure that we learn from the past and take advantage of all our strengths which the other sports don't have. They have always labelled us as the 'sleeping giant'. It's a boring label because we have never been able to capitalise.

"We are structured for success. We are a commercially driven organisation which means we need to invest more money into the game and we are now structured in a way to deliver. I'm not suggesting we are better than the AFL or NRL—they are great sports—but we are in a unique position. We're the global game and there is no reason we cannot be the same in Australia. It's going to take time and we have to be realistic. But we are on the path to get there and we should not be ashamed of that."

The VAR system is detested by the vast majority. It has not improved the decision-making process and ruined the game as a free-flowing spectacle. Since the league is not legally bound to keep it, why do we still have it?

"I've said this before. We are still in the season where VAR is in play and all things related to the game including VAR will be reviewed in the off-season. I see a lot of discontent that needs to be taken seriously. It's far from perfect, it needs a lot of attention and it needs to improve. And if it can't improve we need to consider removing it. I'm not going to cast aspersions on it because any decision we will make about VAR will require proper analysis."

But most fans don't want VAR tweaked ... they just want it out of the game.

"With all respect, yours might be a straw poll of opinions. That's not the way I do research. I go through a proper process of speaking to players and coaches. Some remember life without it and prefer this, others don't. It's all opinion. We need to have proper diligence and test all opinions and look at alternatives, not just ask people you know."

Footy finals are part of Australia's culture yet teams finishing first past the post are recognised worldwide as champions. With the grand final winners deprived of a spot in the ACL Champions League do the end-of-season playoffs have a future?

"It's simple. The finals are the peak of interest in our code in this country. We need to celebrate what is great and unique about our football and the finals are a fantastic experience. It is where our attendances grow and when new people are exposed to our game. So we will keep that as a key part of football in this country."

The A-League trio's withdrawal from the ACL will affect Australia's ranking. If the worse comes to the worst we might be relegated to the AFC Cup. Would we still compete in that tournament?

"Absolutely. We'll be taking part in any competitions we qualify for. At the end of the day, we're about competing and putting Australian football on whatever map we can put it on. If that's the AFC Cup, so be it."

The forced introduction of young gifted players due to the effects of the pandemic has been one of the highlights of the season. Will the new league reconsider the merits of spending less on foreigners?

"I think what you see at the moment is not so much the impact of COVID but the maturation of the investment the 12 clubs have made in their academies. We took control of the elite pathway about six years ago and we are now seeing the fruit of our investment. So now we are seeing a wave of amazing young talent that we are producing regularly.

"Of course, we need to find a balance between the local and foreign components. Can you imagine how much a young player could learn from the way a quality foreigner plays his football?"

Will the quota of five foreigners per club stay?

"We have no intention of changing that anytime soon. That's something we would have to work out with the FA because it would impact the national interest. But like everything else, over time you review things and if you think there is a reason, you change your actions accordingly."

The Big Interviews

One of the most enjoyable and rewarding aspects of being a football writer is the opportunity to get the occasional one-on-one interview with a big player or a top personality.

Uncompromising defender Claudio Gentile opened up on a magnificent career for club and country and admitted that accusations of being a dirty player do not sit well with him.

Hitman Gentile goes on the attack
3 March 1992

They didn't call Claudio Gentile a 'hitman' for nothing. Italy's 1982 World Cup hero was one of the hardest men in football.

But love him or hate him, Gentile can look back on a marvellous career which has given him just about everything.

The Libyan-born defender is one of a select number of players to have won just about every honour the game can bestow at club or international level.

Apart from the World Cup, Gentile has won the European Cup, Cup Winners' Cup, UEFA Cup, world club championship and six Italian league titles with Juventus.

But no matter how successful or fulfilling his career might have been, Gentile will always be remembered as an uncompromising and ruthless stopper.

Gentile, 38, is in Sydney as a member of the Club Italia veterans side which will meet a Marconi selection in an exhibition game at Marconi tonight.

"Yes, it's unfair and it hurts," Gentile was telling me the other day.

"It's a tag which had stuck with me throughout my career.

"But what many people do not realise is that I have played in 450 Italian league games, 70 internationals and 110 European club matches and I've never been sent off in my life.

"I was not a dirty player and I've never ever hurt anyone.

"Sure, I was tough and I had to be because it was my job to mark dangerous players out of a game. But I was also fair and all my opponents admit this."

Gentile invariably ended up winning nearly all his ferocious duels with the world's greatest stars.

His job as an Italian-style stopper was simply to stop his direct opponent from scoring.

But he often went one better—sometimes he even stopped them from touching the ball.

Gentile was a superb and highly motivated athlete and a defender who stuck to his job—and man—with unflappable discipline.

His crunching tackles never broke any legs but they often ripped the heart out of the toughest and most hardened forwards.

In Italy he enjoyed celebrity status, even though he was not endowed with the skills normally associated with the finest players.

There is one aspect in football, however, which he has not been able to overcome—the workings of the football agent.

Until a few years ago a player in Italy could open his local paper and discover he'd been transferred.

Amazingly, deals were made by clubs and agents without the consent of the players themselves.

"Fortunately this practice was abolished in the mid-1980s but the agents in Italy are still very much a powerful part of our system," Gentile said.

"I'm not sure what happens abroad but our agents are ripping us off and also sending the clubs broke.

"We've tried to do something about it but we have failed. The middle men are very powerful in Italy."

Gentile, who quit competitive football four years ago, has taken up residence in the picturesque town of Como and works as a talent scout for Juventus.

"Juventus are the sort of club that appreciate good service from their players," he said.

The Turinese giants owe a lot to the Zoffs, Cabrinis, Tardellis, Scireas, Platinis and Bonieks for their magnificent run in the 1980s.

But they probably would not have won half as many honours without the man many fans hated but who most coaches would have loved to have on their side.

* * *

'QUOTE UNQUOTE'

Franco Baresi was a star attraction when AC Milan made a short tour of Australia in 1993. I caught up with the 'Rossoneri' legend in Sydney.

Why Baresi will always be a Milan legend
18 June 1993

AC Milan supporters have every reason to adore defender Franco Baresi.

The long-serving capitano, who has not played for any other club, has acquired legendary status at the co-tenants of the San Siro stadium.

Fans all the world appreciate loyalty, you see.

And Baresi's immense popularity is due no doubt to the fact that he did not abandon the club when it was twice relegated in the early 1980s.

"To me Milan is not just my job but my second family," Baresi said.

"I grew up in Milan and I've been playing there for 18 years since I was 14."

Baresi will long be remembered as one of Milan's all-time greats.

And his sterling services have not gone unrewarded.

The swashbuckling international sweeper is reported to be on a salary of $1.6 million—that's just the basic—which makes him and striker Marco Van Basten Milan's highest-paid players.

Baresi, who matter-of-factly declared that Serie A was much harder to win than the European Cup, is still trying to come to terms with the club's shock loss to Marseille in the 1993 final.

Milan had won each and every match on their way to the final in Munich and were hot favourites to land the trophy with the big ears but a headed goal from Basile Boli dashed their hopes.

"That 1–0 defeat was the biggest disappointment of my career," he said only days after playing in the final.

"It was as shattering a blow as Italy's defeat on penalties against Argentina in the 1990 World Cup semi-finals.

"But I've also had a few great moments, mind you. I will never forget, for example, my first European Cup win in 1989 when we beat Steaua Bucharest 4–0 in Barcelona."

At 33, Baresi is past his peak and he knows it.

He is finding it increasingly harder to contain younger and faster players, hence his apparent propensity to commit more fouls, although he won't admit it.

Early this year he was sent off in a World Cup qualifier in Malta for handling the ball when caught out of position.

"Actually, I have mellowed a bit the last few years," he said with a mischievous grin. "You should have seen me when I was a younger and less mature defender."

* * *

Diego Maradona's comeback from the drug-related suspension for the 1994 World Cup playoff with Australia created world headlines. He was happy to give me an exclusive interview a week before the first leg in Sydney.

Don't let the game die, pleads Maradona
25 October 1993

Argentine ace Diego Maradona yesterday made an impassioned plea to world football's governing body FIFA "to do something to save the game".

The South American genius, who will make his international competitive comeback against Australia on Sunday after a 15-month suspension over cocaine use, warned that unless football changed direction it would self-destruct.

"The game has become too big with too many interests attached," he said in fluent Italian.

"There is too much money at stake.

"There is also too much pressure on footballers and it's not fun anymore.

"We simply cannot continue to destroy the game."

Maradona said the truly skilful players were being gradually kicked out of the game.

"It's not just me but other great strikers like (Marco) Van Basten are not being allowed to play good football," he said.

"Coaches these days are putting on the park six or seven defenders with the sole intention of destroying the gifted players.

"These coaches should be promoting attacking players that are capable of putting the ball in the net."

Maradona, looking incredibly fit and relaxed in the lead-up to his comeback to the Argentine side, said he felt it was his duty to help his country in its hour of need.

After a 5-0 drubbing by Colombia in a World Cup qualifier in Buenos Aires that forced Argentina into a playoff with the Socceroos, public opinion forced coach Alfio Basile to pick 'El Pibe de Oro' (Golden Boy) in his squad.

"Whoever wears the Argentine jersey—not just me but any player—has a big duty towards his country and I felt a responsibility to play," he said.

Whatever anyone says about the controversial Maradona, his patriotic fervour is beyond question and well documented.

He is known to have played for his country several times while carrying injuries.

Earlier this year he publicly berated Argentine international Fernando Redondo for quitting the national team in 1989 when he was a fringe player.

Redondo, who is expected to join Maradona and the rest of the Argentine squad tomorrow after playing for Tenerife in the Spanish first division early today, had made himself unavailable in order to concentrate on his economics degree.

For a while the two players were not on speaking terms but are understood to have made up.

"I am feeling great and as well as I have felt for a long time," Maradona said.

"The will to train and play has returned and it's great to be back in Argentina's football environment."

At his peak Maradona was considered as great a player as immortals Alfredo di Stefano, Pele, Franz Beckenbauer and Johan Cruyff.

Although he would not be drawn into making a comparison between him and the other heroes, he said each one had his own special characteristics.

"No, I wouldn't say I was the best but I'd like to think that I was a different type of player," he said.

"You see, I have a different feel for the game.

"I always believed football should be played with fun and without too much drama and pressure."

Although Maradona would be the first to admit that he is past his peak, he still has enough pride left in his lean and compact body to leave yet another mark on the game he has adorned for so many years.

His determination to get back to peak fitness after his long suspension has drawn admiration from many quarters.

Hence the obvious question: How did he lose so much weight in such a short time?

"Well, it's a long story but I was determined to succeed, mainly with my diet," he said.

"I can tell you, shedding so many kilos is very difficult, especially since there are so many good things to eat."

Yes, the hunger is still there all right.

* * *

Gary Lineker, the leading scorer in the 1986 World Cup, explained how he was frozen out of the England team by 'no frills' manager Graham Taylor.

Taylor drove me out of England team, says Lineker
11 October 1994

Prolific striker Gary Lineker claims former England manager Graham Taylor forced him and other stars out of the national team to create a no-frills side of multi-purpose workhorses.

Lineker, who is in Australia for pre-season with his Japanese side Nagoya Gampus Eight, said he always sensed he had little future with Taylor.

"I just did not fit into his plans," Lineker, 34, said.

"He believed I was from another era and made it clear he wanted his own hand-picked men on board."

Lineker conceded he was stunned at being replaced in the crucial match against Sweden in the 1992 European Championship, when he needed only one goal to equal Bobby Charlton's record of 49.

"Taylor said it was a tactical change because I was not holding the ball up. Anyway, it was his decision and he had to live or die by it," he said.

"Of course, I was disappointed but I forgot all about it after two days.

"There are more important things in life than worrying about being replaced in a football match.

"After all, I've had a fairly successful career."

Lineker never played again for England.

Soon afterwards, disillusioned at the way he was treated, he headed east in search of the rising yen and signed a two-year contract with the Nagoya club.

Lineker said Taylor's attitude forced creative players like Bryan Robson, Peter Beardsley and Chris Waddle away from the national team.

"They were just frozen out," he said.

Taylor was not the only coach with whom Lineker had problems.

He also spoke of a strained relationship with Johan Cruyff during his three-year stint with Barcelona from 1986.

"Cruyff wanted me to play on the right wing, which is not my position," he explained.

"Playing on the wing is much easier but I'm a central striker and I get a buzz from scoring. And you don't get many goals when you play out wide."

So did he talk to the manager?

"You don't complain with Cruyff... you just do as you're told," he said, deadpan.

Lineker, who is renowned for his tact and diplomacy in his dealings with the media, also hinted at a personality clash with the famous Dutchman.

"I respected him as a coach but he has a big ego and he is not the sort of bloke I would like to have as a close friend," he said.

With the 1990 World Cup around the corner and his England centre-forward position at risk because he was not scoring enough goals, he went back to his homeland where he resumed his extraordinary scoring feats with Tottenham Hotspur.

*   *   *

Eccentric Colombian goalkeeper Rene Higuita was rebounding from his own 'annus horribilis' when he visited Australia with the national team.

Higuita reveals his torment over Escobar murder
11 February 1995

Colourful Colombia goalkeeper Rene Higuita, the man they call 'The Madman', is still trying to come to terms with a horrible 12 months that nearly cost him his sanity.

Higuita, who is in Australia for the two-match series with the Socceroos, said 1994 was the worst year he could remember.

He spent the first part of the year completing a six-month jail term for his illegal involvement in the release of a kidnapped girl.

Then after losing his place in the national team, he watched helplessly as his country went from one disaster to another in the World Cup in the United States.

And to cap it all he was horrified to learn of the murder of one of his best mates, Andres Escobar, after he scored the most notorious own goal in football history.

Higuita, 29, told of the anguish he suffered when he learned of the killing of Escobar.

The tall defender could so easily have laid low for a few weeks after Colombia's World Cup flop in which he committed an own goal in a key match against the USA.

However, he chose to have a night out with friends and was gunned down outside a Medellin club after an argument.

"The whole affair was very sad," Higuita said.

"Andres was a very good friend of mine and a teammate in Colombia's junior and senior team for many years.

"When he returned home from the USA he rang me to say hello and have a chat but we never managed to get together before he died."

Escobar's death has been linked to betting syndicates and a drug cartel.

Higuita denied that playing for Colombia was a dangerous job, considering the forces that seem to have infiltrated the game.

"I play football because I love it and I have never felt any pressures from outside the game," he said.

"Some of my colleagues have spoken about this and that but I myself have never come across anything of the sort."

Higuita rose to international fame in the late 1980s through his extravagant looks and unconventional approach towards goalkeeping.

He often causes consternation by leaving the penalty area to take part in general play.

Still sporting long, black, curly locks and a thick moustache, the Nacional goalkeeper said yesterday he won't change his adventurous style.

"I've worked hard and with the help of God I want to have a second career," he said.

Higuita admitted it would be hard for Colombia to recover from their World Cup shambles.

Colombia were among the favourites to win the trophy but two shocking displays gave them an early ticket home.

"We've got to bury the past and start afresh," he said.

"Our next big tests are the Copa America and the 1998 World Cup qualifiers."

Higuita is well known for his love of children's welfare. Early in the week he made it a point to visit a terminally ill child in a Brisbane hospital.

But when he intervened in a kidnapping case and helped a friend pay a ransom for his daughter he was convicted and jailed for six months.

*   *   *

Salvatore Schillaci, the man who came from nowhere and took the World Cup by storm, was nearing the end of his career when I had a chat with him in Sydney.

Battler Schillaci's career drawing to a close
28 February 1995

For a whole month during Italia '90 striker Salvatore Schillaci held the soccer world in the palm of his hand: whatever he touched turned into gold.

His scoring feats in the World Cup made him the darling of Italy's passionate tifosi.

Schillaci, who hails from Palermo in Sicily, became an instant hero in a classic fairytale of a brave battler who was given the chance of his life and he took it.

Pictures of this cheeky little skinhead with bulging eyes who came out of nowhere to steal the show were beamed across the world.

His predator's instincts helped Italy secure third place in the tournament on home soil.

Schillaci, 30, now plays for Japanese club Jubilo Iwata, who are currently in pre-season training in Sydney.

But he is struggling to maintain his high scoring standard in the J.League.

"I'm having a good time in a fascinating country," he told me yesterday.

"But it's very hard because the standard is getting higher."

Schillaci admits he misses Italy and the pressure-cooker atmosphere of Serie A.

"It was a tough decision to leave Inter. It took me months to make up my mind but I had to secure my future," he said.

"I also needed a new challenge and I wanted to experience foreign football and another country but I feel a deep sense of nostalgia towards Italy and its football.

"I've got one year of my contract to go and come September we'll see what happens."

Schillaci played for Juventus and Inter for four seasons before seeking greener pastures at the end of his career.

But he is still a big fan of the Turin side.

"It looks like this is Juventus's year," he said.

"They seem to have got their act together and should go on and win the title.

"I sincerely wish them the best of luck."

Schillaci's worldwide profile in 1990 was so high that in Australia they even named a horse after him.

"I was watching the World Cup on SBS and we named our new gelding after Italy's deadly finisher," said champion sprinter Schillaci's part-owner Alan Bell.

*   *   *

The great Pele is revered in his native Brazil but that did not stop World Cup-winning captain Carlos Dunga from having a go at 'O Rei' for his criticism of modern-day footballers.

Brazil skipper Dunga blasts Pele
21 February 1996

Brazil's World Cup-winning captain Carlos Dunga yesterday took a swipe at the great Pele for slamming football's modern-day 'mercenaries'.

Dunga, who is in Sydney for pre-season training with his Japanese club Jubilo Iwata, said Pele had no right to criticise professional players for trying to better themselves.

Pele has often spoken out against Brazilian stars who "change clubs for a dollar more" or leave their country to make a quick buck in Europe or Japan.

"I can't understand why Pele is complaining," Dunga said yesterday.

"He was always the highest paid player at Santos and wherever he played.

"Towards the end of his career—when Santos could not meet his demands—he went to the United States to play for New York Cosmos.

"And he was the first to say players should be free to move from one club to another without a transfer fee, so why is he so concerned now that we are trying to get the best deal for ourselves?

"It's a free market. What you earn depends on how good you are. It's the same as in any sport."

Dunga, who scored one of the penalties that helped Brazil beat Italy in the 1994 World Cup final shootout, also spoke about rising star Juninho's rough initiation to English football with struggling Middlesbrough.

Juninho rose to fame with marvellous performances in the Umbro Cup in England and Copa America in Uruguay last year but he is having problems in leaving his mark in an increasingly competitive Premier League.

"Juninho is a great young player but he has to be patient," Dunga said.

"It takes a while to get used to a different environment and a contrasting style of football.

"Next year will be much better for him. The important thing is to be able to adapt."

Dunga should know. The 32-year-old midfield maestro has played in Brazil, Italy, Germany and Japan in a sparkling career spanning 15 years and nine clubs.

And yet he is still eager to win one major honour that has eluded him—an Olympic Games gold medal.

He is not allowed to play in the qualifying series being played in Argentina but will be eligible in Atlanta in 1996 as one of the allowed three over-age players.

* * *

'QUOTE UNQUOTE'

Michel Platini, one of football's all-time greats, said he was not overly dismayed by France's failure to reach the final of the 1982 World Cup when they had West Germany on the ropes.

Platini looks back fondly at French folly
15 June 1999

Seville 1982 is not something French football fans would remember fondly.

A World Cup semi-final defeat against West Germany that France should have won easily went horribly wrong.

What should have been French football's finest hour turned into a nightmare as Germany came back from the dead to sneak into the final with a considerable dose of good fortune.

So it came as a huge surprise that Michel Platini, the greatest player France has produced, regards that terrible night in Spain as the highlight of his magnificent playing career.

Platini, 44 next week, is a FIFA advisor nowadays and was in Sydney last week for the Socceroos versus All-Stars match.

"It was without doubt the high point of my career," he said.

"To have taken part in one of the greatest matches in history was a privilege because I lived through two hours of football excellence nobody will ever experience again.

"It was magical. Okay, we lost, but France had been losing for a very long time so it was no big deal, really.

"If the referee had sent off Toni Schumacher for felling Patrick Battiston and given us a penalty for the same foul we would have been in the final but it was not meant to be.

"I will never forget the sight of my devastated teammates weeping like kids in the dressing room after the game.

"They were not tears of disappointment but a release from the high drama and tension."

France, with Platini, Alain Giresse, Jean Tigana and Luis Fernandez dominating, were leading 3-1 in extra time when the seemingly beaten Germans staged one of their trademark recoveries to take the match to a shootout which they won.

The French, after playing so beautifully all night, were left to curse their rotten luck and hang around for the platonic match for third place against Poland.

"There was some good to come out of our misfortune, however," Platini said.

"It made us realise we had a wonderful side and that we could compete with the world's best."

Indeed, only two years later Platini's troops gave France its first major honour when 'Les Bleus' beat Spain 2-0 in the European Championship final at the Parc des Princes in Paris.

Giresse, who also was in Sydney for the weekend game, said France lost their epic semi-final because the team was relatively young and inexperienced.

"We could have closed up the game when we were 3-1 up but we wanted to keep attacking," Giresse, 46, said.

Platini, who was one of the finest players to grace a football field, made a name for himself as a free-scoring inside-forward at Nancy and Saint-Etienne.

His ability to carve up openings with inventive passing and find the net with inch-perfect free kicks made the world sit up and take notice.

It did not take him long to break into the national team and when he played what he terms as "the best game of my career" in a friendly against Italy in Paris in 1981, Juventus came along with the sort of contract the Italians offer only to real superstars.

Platini spent five superlative years in Turin and made Juve the best team in the world in the mid-80s.

He also helped himself to three European Footballer of the Year awards.

Juve had a star-studded team that included six Italians who won the 1982 World Cup but Platini, the man they called 'Il Divino', was president Gianni Agnelli's favourite player.

"Well, he wanted me at all costs to replace Liam Brady and paid me a lot of money to make Juve a champion side and I think I did so," he said.

Platini, who used to caress the ball as if it were a piece of bone china, made and scored many goals for club and country.

So which was his greatest?

"The best goal I ever scored was disallowed," he said.

"It came in late 1985 in Tokyo during Juve's world club championship match with Argentinos Juniors."

Being the natural showman, Platini then gave me an impromptu demonstration of how he scored that 'goal'.

He showed me how he controlled the ball on his chest, beat two men without letting the ball hit the ground and found the top corner of the net.

"It was just beautiful but it was disallowed for a passive offside infringement by Sergio Brio," he said.

"A Singaporean linesman put his flag up. You know, I could have killed him."

* * *

'QUOTE UNQUOTE'

FIFA president Sepp Blatter urged Australia to go for the World Cup after it staged a marvellous Olympics in Sydney.

Blatter says Australia should go for World Cup
26 September 2000

FIFA president Sepp Blatter yesterday urged Australia to throw in its hat for the World Cup.

If Australia can handle an Olympic Games, it can stage a World Cup, he said.

"After organising such a fantastic Olympics, Australia is absolutely and without any shadow of doubt entitled to go for the World Cup," Blatter said in his plush suite at a Sydney hotel.

"What the Australians have done is marvellous.

"If you can stage an event with 10,000 athletes, 10,000 officials and 20,000 media personnel, why can't you cater for a much smaller event?

"The World Cup comprises only 32 teams so we are talking about fewer than a thousand athletes.

"It is therefore much easier to hold a World Cup than an Olympics as long as you have the venues available."

Blatter said Australia had big stadia in major cities and the ones he had seen so far in Sydney 2000 were a credit to the country.

"New technology today allows you to create a football pitch elsewhere and put on a ground whenever you need to," he said.

"They did this in Canberra with great success."

Blatter said the 'Charlie Dempsey debacle', that gave the 2006 World Cup to Germany at the expense of his favourite South Africa and undermined his influence as head of football, would not compromise Oceania's chances of holding the game's biggest tournament.

"I'm a football man and you have to accept that you win some games and you lose some," he said.

"And in sport you have to be good loser, don't you?

"I am not a man of revenge and I can assure Oceania that the whole saga is already forgotten.

"It was not Mr Dempsey alone anyway. There were other factors.

"We are a democracy and we recognise that every member of FIFA's executive committee had a right to vote as he wished.

"I have nothing against Mr Dempsey. He even will be my guest in Sydney tonight.

"The affair has done the Australians no harm at all.

"FIFA has now ratified the rotation system for the tournament so Oceania will have a right to stage the cup."

And in the clearest indication yet that the two-yearly World Cup is still very much on the agenda, Blatter said: "We shall see now whether a four-yearly World Cup is the right way to go, bearing in mind that the six confederations will have to wait 24 years to hold a series.

"By the end of the year we will have a clearer idea of where we're going. That's when the strategic committee of FIFA will present its recommendation."

This committee, incidentally, is the only one chaired directly by the president.

* * *

England's World Cup-winning hero Geoff Hurst expressed his candid views on the heated 'club versus country' debate.

England always came first, says Hurst
10 February 2003

England's 1966 World Cup hero Geoff Hurst has joined the widening club versus country debate by declaring the national team always came first in his entire professional career.

Hurst, who scored a hat-trick in England's 4–2 win over West Germany in the final, is in Australia on holiday at Sanctuary Cove, soaking up the sun and playing as many rounds of golf as possible in a bid to improve his handicap of 18.

He flew down to Sydney at the weekend to have a look at the NSW Soccer Federation's set-up at Glenwood, the famed football factory that produced Harry Kewell and Brett Emerton.

"In my day if anyone at West Ham said to me I shouldn't play for England I would have told them where to go," Hurst, now 61, said.

"There is no greater honour in football or any other sport than representing your country. Most of the boys I played with felt the same way too.

"The club versus country argument has become a big conflict now but it existed to a lesser degree in my time too.

"If you were only a national team squad player, your club manager might have told you 'look, you're not likely to play and we've got a big league game coming up' but if you were a regular international player for six years as I was I would have told them 'no way, I'm off'.

"It's a bit different now. Clubs are more powerful and have more money and greater control over their highly paid stars.

"Clubs don't like friendly international matches. Especially now that there is so much competitive football.

"Managers say 'it's just a friendly, you can't play in a friendly'.

"But you've got to have friendlies because that's when you find out if a player is good enough to play for his country at competitive level."

As Hurst watched some of NSW's young players hone their skills, he expressed his admiration for Australian football's progress, as evidenced by the growing number of Australians who play their trade in Europe.

He refuted suggestions that the lack of a real football culture in Australia was a stumbling block.

"You can overcome that if the people running the game get better at club, state and national level," he said.

"If Australia produces 11 Harry Kewells and starts beating teams regularly, then the press will start taking notice.

"Soccer has to look at what cricket has done with its academy. If so many thousands of children play soccer over here, what's to stop Australia from producing the right players and being successful?"

* * *

Brazil legend Pele would not be drawn into the 'who was the best' debate when we had a little tête-à-tête in Sydney.

Legendary Pele a champion on and off the pitch
7 March 2006

So was Pele the world's greatest footballer of all time or wasn't he?

The popular Brazilian is widely regarded as the game's finest and most accomplished player.

Yet many contend that Argentine heroes Alfredo di Stefano and Diego Maradona are entitled to the same accolade.

Pele covered himself in glory during a magnificent career that earned him three World Cups in 1958, 1962 and 1970 and gave him everlasting fame and fortune.

Di Stefano never played in a World Cup but led the legendary Real Madrid side that won five straight European Cups from 1956, scoring in every final.

Maradona inspired Argentina to the 1986 World Cup and helped Napoli win two

Italian championships.

When Pele, 65, lobbed into town last week on promotional work for MasterCard, the question had to be put to him, albeit in a roundabout way.

"It's not polite to make comparisons," he replied when asked who was his second best player of all time.

"Especially since everybody seems to remember the top strikers and not the top defenders.

"I'll tell you one thing, though. Those Argentines were always challenging me.

"In the 50s and 60s they claimed that Di Stefano was better than me.

"Then when he quit they compared me with Omar Sivori (who played with John Charles for Juventus in the 60s) and in the 80s they brought up Maradona.

"What Argentina should do first is make up its mind as to who was its best player … then we can have a debate (chuckles).

"I mean no offence … I have lots of friends in Argentina."

Having sorted that one out, the 'Black Pearl' was asked if he would have had any problems fitting into the Brazil side that is strongly favoured to win the World Cup in July.

"Today's footballers have it easy," he said with a blend of protest and mischief.

"They have much better facilities and conditions. And what about the protection they get from referees?

"You can't go anywhere near an opponent today because you get a yellow or red card."

Pele is believed to have scored more than 1200 goals in his stellar career that spanned three decades.

Yet when asked which one gave him most pleasure, for once he was lost for words.

After a while he said: "Perhaps it was the solo goal I scored against Sweden in the 1958 World Cup final as a 17-year-old because it made my career."

Pele spent an entire afternoon giving interviews and when my time with the great man was up, he said "ciao amigo" before he was whisked away to yet another engagement.

Pele looks drawn and tired these days, yet he handles the media hounds who have been wanting a piece of him for decades with the same enthusiasm he has shown ever since he became a celebrity in the late 1950s.

He still exudes genuine warmth and friendliness and has a beaming smile for everyone.

Pele may or may not have been the greatest of all time … but as a human being he will always be a champion.

* * *

'QUOTE UNQUOTE'

Star striker Gianfranco Zola admitted during a Sydney visit that Italy were lucky to beat Australia at the 2006 World Cup.

Zola defends Italian image after 'that' dive
31 December 2006

Little master Gianfranco Zola yesterday relived Italy's great escape against Australia at the 2006 World Cup and declared: "We were gone, then we got lucky."

The Italian striker revealed the grave concerns many Italians had about the outcome of the knockout clash after defender Marco Materazzi was sent off early in the second half.

"We all thought we were gone. Australia had a good tournament and gave us a very hard game," Zola, 40, said in Sydney, where he was invited to play in an exhibition match in his honour between Marconi and APIA at Marconi Stadium on Friday night.

"We really feared the worst, more so after we were a man down.

"The Socceroos took control and Italy were not playing too well but we were lucky to get through because of the late penalty.

"That match actually was the turning point of our campaign because we showed how hungry we were to succeed.

"We won the World Cup basically because we wanted it most."

Many Australian fans still resent the controversial way the Socceroos were kicked out of the event in the round of 16.

Fabio Grosso's dive that fooled the referee become the most talked about simulation since Meg Ryan's in *When Harry Met Sally*.

"My first reaction was that it was a penalty but after watching the replay I had to admit it was a bad decision," Zola said.

Lucas Neill, who was judged to have fouled Grosso, has talked of his disgust at Italy's so-called culture of doing "whatever it takes" to win.

Zola, however, retorted it was wrong and unfair to brand Italian players as cheats.

"Italian football produces many great and fair players and others who would not hesitate to bend the rules," he protested.

"Lucas must have been deeply frustrated to say that and I can understand him.

"But not all Italians are like that and, besides, we are not the only ones who do it."

Zola, who lit up the Premiership in a seven-year spell with Chelsea, is from that breed of footballer who puts his word ahead of money.

And when Chelsea owner Roman Ambramovich threw his dodgy roubles at the striker in a desperate bid to make him stay on in 2003, Zola said 'no' because he had promised Serie A club Cagliari he would sign for them.

"My contract with Chelsea was up and we failed to agree on a new deal," Zola, who hails from Sardinia, explained.

"I then talked to Cagliari and we agreed terms. There was no contract, just a verbal agreement to meet at a given day to seal the deal.

"The night before, Abramovich made me a better offer but it was too late because I had given my word to Cagliari."

Promoters B & B Sporting Enterprises had no doubts that Zola would honour his commitment and come to Sydney.

In a public relations coup that shot former giants Marconi and APIA back into an albeit fleeting limelight, Zola drew a decent crowd when he played one half for each team, showing glimpses of his best days before he ran out of puff.

Marconi scored twice in each half to win 4–0.

The Socceroos Greats

This is a selection of interviews with several of Australia's finest players for the long-running series on *The World Game* entitled *Socceroos Greats—Where are they now?*

> *Talking to Kevin O'Neill, Australia's oldest Socceroo, made me realise that football had changed beyond recognition from the game the miner-cum-footballer used to play almost a century ago.*

O'Neill drove for seven hours to play football
11 May 2021

Kevin O'Neill, who is recognised by historians as the oldest living Socceroo, gave a rare insight into his long amateur career that started while Australia was at war.

O'Neill, 95, said he was privileged to be able to play the game he loved even though he hardly ever got paid and had to make huge sacrifices just to realise his dreams and aspirations.

O'Neill spent most of his career playing for Cessnock in the Northern NSW federation and he also represented Australia 12 times in full internationals or 'Tests', as certain international matches were known back then.

He was simply an international player those days. The 'Socceroos' nickname would come much later.

He also played for two years with glamour club Prague in Sydney but, since he worked in the coal mines in and around Newcastle, he preferred to live in his hometown of Cessnock and commute to training and games.

"I had a Holden those days and it did not worry me at all to drive to Sydney on a Sunday morning, play the game and come back home to be ready for work on Monday," O'Neill said from his home at a retirement village in Cessnock, which is a gateway to the Hunter Valley.

"The problems arose when we had midweek Ampol Cup games in Sydney. It was common for me to finish work at the mine at three, drive to Sydney, play the evening game, drive back home and arrive after midnight, then go to work the next morning at seven.

"That was very hard and for that reason I used to take a friend of mine with me just to keep me company, especially for the trip home.

"The drive to Sydney and back usually took about seven hours. The reason I did it was because of my love of the game. It had to be.

"I never really got paid to play for Cessnock because I was a pure amateur. It actually cost me money to play. On a couple of occasions I got paid six pounds at the end of the year to cover my expenses. It was not even enough to buy a pair of boots so I put it in the kids' money box.

"When I was at Prague, the club provided boots for us. The club also told us at the end of the championship-winning season in 1959 that they were flying us to Melbourne to play two friendly matches. After playing the first game I walked off the field and felt I was not in the best shape to play the second game the next day.

"I was told if I did not play I would not get the bonus of 30 pounds. So I said to the club that I would play even with one leg to get the cash—and I did."

O'Neill was happy to share some of his experiences of a football world that cannot be any more removed from that of today's game.

You grew up in the Hunter Valley, where there are as many wineries as football clubs. What attracted you to the game?

"I lived opposite the Cessnock ground and I always played football when I was young. The vineyards were never a temptation. I don't drink and I don't smoke."

The first three years of your career in first grade were in wartime. What was that like?

"I was 17 in 1942 and playing juniors for Cessnock and a year later I was in first grade for Kurri Kurri. To be honest, the war did not really affect me up here in Cessnock. I actually wanted to enlist but my mother would not let me sign up, first because my brother was already in the war and, secondly, I had a good protected job in the coal-mining industry."

You played most of your 22-year career in the Hunter except for two seasons with Prague.

"NSW Football had a breakaway in 1944 and the strongest teams from the Newcastle area went to the new competition. I was asked to join West Wallsend because I was told the club would make me a better player. I joined up on one condition: that when the breakaway competition was over I would go to Cessnock."

The Cessnock Eagle *newspaper once described you as one of the most popular footballers in the game. What type of player were you?*

"I was free and easy. And pretty versatile too. At Cessnock I played left-half, centre-half, right-back and even on the wing for the national team. I used to like playing in different positions."

What are your best memories from your 14-year 'association' with Cessnock?

"We were the best side for several years in the NNSW federation and the 1956 team that won the championship was the best I have ever played in. We had seven internationals. On our day we would beat anybody."

You achieved the honour of winning the NSW championship with Prague and had the privilege of playing alongside Leo Baumgartner. What do you remember of that team and that very special player?

"Leo always wanted the ball at his feet. If you put it a metre away from him he'd be cross with you. But by the same token I would go crook on him if he did not give me the ball where I wanted it. So it was even-steven, I suppose. We had a great side at Prague but I reckon our Cessnock team of 1956 would have held its own against Prague."

How often did you train with your clubs and what was a typical training session like?

"We used to train twice a week, usually for a couple of hours, on Tuesdays and Thursdays. We used to first run around the ground a few times, then do some physical exercises and finally play a little game. We never worked on skills because in the first years of my career we did not even have coaches. I always wore bandages at training and in matches to protect my ankles and after training or a game I would run cold water on them and make sure they were okay."

You were selected in the Australian team that toured Africa in 1950. Your first football trip abroad must have been a great experience.

"It was just a terrific experience, something I would not have gained if I went on my own. The situation in South Africa at the time (apartheid had been in force for two years) meant that we could not associate with non-whites.

"I remember catching a plane from Williamtown to Adelaide, then on to Fremantle, from where the whole team caught a boat to Cape Town. I was sick all the way and so pleased to finally get my feet on firm ground. From Cape Town we flew to Johannesburg and funnily enough some of the players who were not sick on the boat got sick on the plane.

"We played against Rhodesia (now Zimbabwe) twice and South Africa four times. We won two matches and lost two against the South Africans and I think the tour leaders wanted to play a fifth 'Test' but the hosts declined so we came home."

Despite the fact that you were one of the most prominent players of your generation—you captained the national team three times—you missed out on the 1956 Olympics squad. What happened there?

"I think I know the reason. My wife was not well in the months leading up to the Games and I refused to play in a trial match between NSW and Victoria in Melbourne because I had to look after her. So I was not picked. NSW selectors tried to get me in to no avail."

Would that be the biggest disappointment in your career?

"I don't know. I did have another huge disappointment in 1948. I was selected to tour New Zealand, where we were to play four international matches. After a trial match at Wallsend, my workmates told me 'pack your bags, you're going on tour ... you can't miss out'. But I did miss out because an official from Queensland nominated a player from his state for my position and the selectors went with him. Those days the national team was picked by representatives from all the federations."

In 1958, you played four times for Australia against the touring Blackpool side that had Stanley Matthews on the right wing. Are you glad you were a right-back and did not have to face him?

"Blackpool played five matches in Australia but I did not play in their first game at the Sports Ground in Sydney, so I went to watch Matthews play. Yes, you could say I was lucky not to have to deal with Matthews but, mind you, their South African left winger Bill Perry (who scored Blackpool's winning goal in the FA Cup final against Bolton Wanderers) was quite a handful, too."

Are you still in contact with any of the surviving players of your time?

"Out of the Cessnock team of 1956 there are only two others left: Jimmy Porteus and Billy Thompson, whom I sometimes visit."

* * *

Former Socceroos captain Les Scheinflug did not hold back when I asked him about the heartbreaking World Cup qualifier versus Iran in Melbourne in 1997.

Scheinflug tells of Socceroos 'sabotage'
10 July 2018

Australia midfielder Les Scheinflug, who captained the national team in their first attempt to qualify for the FIFA World Cup in 1965, said the Socceroos' campaign to reach France '98 was 'sabotaged' by several players who were not fully match fit to face Iran.

Scheinflug, who is now 79, was Soccer Australia's technical director during the campaign headed by English coach Terry Venables.

The Australians were two up and cruising to victory over Iran at the Melbourne Cricket Ground in November 1997 but the team conceded two late goals for a 2–2 draw that crushed their dream of playing in the finals.

Several critics blamed Venables for not trying to protect a 2–0 lead in the latter stages of the game but Scheinflug is not one of them.

"I was technical director during our campaign to reach France," Scheinflug said.

"Many blame Venables for the Socceroos draw that cost us a place in France. They claim we should have defended a two-goal lead but it is the players who were not completely honest with him that are to blame.

"Some of the players who were based abroad and were not playing regularly were not straight with the coach about their match fitness.

"I will not mention names but some of those who faced Iran were not fully match fit. Those days we did not have enough equipment to check the players' physical and medical condition.

"These players let Venables down because they did not give him the right information. The trained but they were not 100 per cent match fit."

German-born Scheinflug, who was never one to mince his words, lives in Sydney's west and spoke at length about the Australian game then and now.

What are you doing now?

"I am very busy looking after my 52-year-old daughter who has Parkinson's Disease. I am not completely cut off from the game because whenever I get time I go to training sessions and local matches to watch some players individually. I also help players and coaches."

You came to Australia in the mid-1950s. What was it like to be a footballer in Australia those days?

"I came out with my father and mother in 1955. I was one of the few who played in the old association before I switched to the new federation. I played for Sydney Prague and we had some very good foreigners like Austrian forwards Leo Baumgartner and Herbert Ninaus.

"I learned a lot from the experienced imports and it was good to have them around. We did not get too much publicity in those 'wogball and sheilas' days. We used to get three paragraphs in the paper and no television but we regularly drew crowds of 15,000 for Ampol Cup matches at our home ground Sydney Athletic Field, which was a good venue.

"Our game was seen as 'foreign' those days. But this never bothered us players. We were young and if somebody talked too much we would tell them where to go so it was never a problem. We just loved the game so we never got involved in anything stupid.

"We were a top side, better technically than today's A-League teams but not so physically. Today's players are essentially workhorses and fitness fanatics but they lack mental intelligence ... when to run or not and when to attack or defend and so on."

Which teams were Prague's biggest rivals in the 1950s and 1960s?

"Our games with Sydney Hakoah and St George Budapest were usually fiercely contested but there were other strong teams later on like Yugal and Auburn. And Melbourne teams were always strong because they too had some top foreigners. Australia was the golden country those days; you found gold in the street."

FIFA banned Australia's football association for three years from 1960 because of its practice of poaching players from Europe and refusing to pay transfer fees. To what extent did this affect the game here?

"Most players hardly ever got paid under the old association, perhaps they got a pound or two at the most. And they never got a clearance from their clubs. Once you signed up you did so for life.

"When the breakaway federation was formed Australia was out of FIFA but the players started getting what they deserved. I made a comfortable living out of the game."

The records show that Australia were two matches away from reaching the 1966 FIFA World Cup but in reality they were miles away when they played North Korea, right?

"I still say that we could have matched the Koreans with better preparation and more knowledge about them and the conditions in neutral Cambodia which is where we played the two matches (6-1 and 3-1). We were in camp for four weeks in north Queensland but we never played any serious preparation matches. All we did was run in the morning and in the afternoon because we knew Phnom Penh would be hot. We never saw the ball."

Tell us more about that eye-opening trip to Cambodia.

"We could have done much better with a coach who could give us more information about the opposition and a doctor who could advise us what not to eat and drink in Cambodia. Seven of us had diarrhoea on the day of the match and we could not get up the next morning. We were buggered.

"As far as I'm concerned I played both games with a badly damaged ankle after I got injured in a meaningless trial against an all-age team in Ingham. We should have played trials against strong teams and it is for this reason that we were outplayed by the Koreans. I scored in both games but we were never in it after the first game."

How come you were overlooked for the 1970 World Cup campaign?

"The ankle injury I suffered in that trial in Ingham affected my career. It was never handled properly and I was given injections to be able to play against Korea. When I came back from Cambodia it got worse and I did not play for nearly a year. I was given more injections but it never healed properly. I missed the trip to Vietnam for the friendship tournament in 1967 and that was it."

Was it hard to watch the Socceroos crash in the playoff against Israel?

"It is always hard to watch the team of your country lose. But it must be said that the players were not well looked after those days. They were semi-professionals but never got any help from the government. They were playing against full-time professionals."

Which was the highlight of your playing career and the low point?

"Playing for Prague, the best team in Australia, is up there among my finest memories. Being involved with the national team was always special. I was captain for the Socceroos' first attempt to reach the World Cup.

"The ankle injury I suffered in that match in Ingham was the low point without doubt. Nobody knew how to fix it and those days you could not have surgery, which was unfortunate. They also gave me cortisone injections after the ankle injury turned into an Achilles tendon problem but that really stuffed me up. I was never the same again."

You have coached Australia at every level from the under-17s to the senior team. Who were the most exciting players you have ever worked with?

"Ned Zelic, Paul Okon, Mark Viduka and Harry Kewell were top performers who had a great attitude and temperament and would never be intimidated by hostile crowds because they were used to playing in front of big crowds every week in Europe. We used to put them under pressure in different conditions at training to find out who could and could not take it but nothing worried them. They were mentally strong players ... they were doers."

What do you think of the Socceroos' performance in Russia?

"I give credit to coach Bert van Marwijk, who should not have been there in the first place, anyway. He had little time to work with but after watching his players in camp in Turkey for three weeks he knew exactly what type of game best suited their qualities. He urged them to play out from the back, keep the ball for as long as possible and sit back for a while when under pressure then go again. But they were unable to score goals, which is nothing new."

How do you rate the state of Australian football?

"The Dutch experiment has failed badly. How much money have we invested in the Dutch in 16 years since Frank Lowy took over and what have we achieved?

"Why did we have to invest $5m on Van Marwijk and his two assistants? Why did we take 40 people from head office to the World Cup? That's about $15m spent on an exercise that could have been done by an Australian coach. After Ange Postecoglou quit last year, FFA should have appointed his assistant Ante Milicic and Tony Popovic.

"We are always screaming for an Australian coach and yet we went for a foreigner. And you know why? Because the FFA since the early days of Lowy believe that any banana from Europe is better than an Aussie coach.

"We should do away with curriculums designed by foreign coaches and concentrate on what we do best and what comes naturally for us.

"Our players are not encouraged to improvise and they have too many defensive duties that stop them from being themselves. Australian players are at their best when they are allowed to have a go in attack but unfortunately these days they are not given the freedom to do so. You cannot play with handcuffs."

Finally, who are the best players you have played with and against?

"Baumgartner was the best. He demanded the ball and would tell you 'go fetch the ball yourself' if it did not come to his feet and when you passed the ball to him he would just go, beat two men and have a crack at goal. He was dynamite.

"I faced England international striker Peter Osgood twice when Chelsea toured Australia in 1965. He scored a smashing goal against us. I also played for NSW against Venables during the same Chelsea tour."

* * *

Flamboyant World Cup striker Adrian Alston
recalled the day he knocked back a firm offer to play in the Bundesliga
to join modest Luton Town.

Alston reveals 'biggest mistake' of his career
3 August 2016

Australia's 1974 World Cup hero Adrian Alston conceded he made the biggest mistake of his footballing career when he snubbed the Bundesliga juggernaut for the rough and tumble English league.

Alston, who is now 68, played a key role in the Socceroos' World Cup campaign and strong performances against East Germany, West Germany and Chile brought him to the attention of some big clubs.

At the time Alston was a semi-professional striker on the books of south coast club Safeway United, who played in the NSW State League.

Hertha Berlin offered him a lucrative package but the English-born striker knocked it back and chose to sign for Luton Town, who had just been promoted to the old first division.

"It was the biggest mistake I ever made," said Alston, who lives in Wollongong and still works with a support group for people with intellectual disability.

"I had three firm offers from Hertha Berlin, Hamburg and Eintracht Frankfurt and I chose Hertha. I will never forget the contract: $40,000 signing-on fee and so much a week plus an apartment until I got myself organised.

"We had agreed terms and a transfer fee had to be arranged between Hertha and Safeway.

"By the time I got back to Australia Luton had expressed an interest because I had scored against them during the Socceroos' world tour the year before and they remembered me, they said.

"Of course, I was thinking my wife and I had family in England and there would be no language barrier. Luton also had just been promoted to the big league and I opted to join them.

"It was a big mistake and Franz Beckenbauer would sum it up perfectly when I met him in America later, and he was spot on.

"He asked me why I went to England when the national team did not even make the (1974) World Cup let alone be a top team.

"He told me everybody in Germany had watched my games and he could not understand why I chose to go to England where nobody had seen me play.

"England were not interested in the World Cup because they did not qualify. In Germany it would have been a massive thing for me and they would have accepted me with no problem at all."

'Noddy' Alston, who played 43 times for the Socceroos, was happy to talk about his club and country career and the great adventure surrounding the 1974 World Cup.

What was Australian football like in the pre-National Soccer League days?

"I came from England. I was an amateur at Preston North End and after a year I was offered a chance to come to Australia. I said, 'Why Australia?' I was told the heavy grounds in England did not suit me because I was a ball player.

"I grew up quite quickly in Australia with the great lifestyle, the nice food and the grounds that suited me. And it went from there.

"The NSW State League comprised almost the whole of the national team and it was a very strong competition. I was playing on the south coast when I was picked for the World Cup."

What do you remember most from the playoff with South Korea for a place in the 1974 World Cup?

"I was speaking to Jimmy Rooney just a few days ago and we both agreed that at the time we did not fully realise what we had achieved until we actually played in the World Cup in Germany.

"To be able to get among the best 16 in the whole world in a tournament like that and be recognised was incredible.

"The game in Hong Kong when we beat South Korea 1–0 obviously sticks in your memory because we were just semi-professional footballers who were not exposed to the world."

The whole qualifying campaign involving tens of thousands of kilometres must have been horrendous.

"Rale Rasic had built a family-type atmosphere within the group from the world tour we had undertaken the year before. We did everything together. And talking about the endless flights ... I am the worst traveller now because of my knees and legs but I always hated flying.

"I remember once I was on a three-seat side of a plane with Col Curran and Atti Abonyi. Curran grabbed a few blankets and lay down on the freezing floor. Atti and myself tried to keep our feet up trying to be comfortable but it was horrendous.

"We spent so much time in the air and in different beds and hotels that our sleeping patterns were always interrupted. Looking back, you ask yourself, 'How did we manage to do that?'"

Tell us about your dribbling move that later would be immortalised by Johan Cruyff as the 'Cruyff turn'.

"I used to do this trick but not very often. I tried it a couple of times in our first match in the World Cup against East Germany and then it came off. I turned the defender, who was rated as one of the best markers in European football, inside out and he just hacked me down.

"West Germany coach Helmut Schoen must have seen me do it when he said I was the most dangerous player in the Socceroos team.

"Johan Cruyff was obviously watching on television too. He must have practised it for five days because five days later he did the same thing against Sweden."

Was playing West Germany at the World Cup the highlight of your career?

"Without a doubt it was ... and getting Beckenbauer's shirt after the match was the icing on the cake.

"Apparently, some museum in Germany wants me to go over there to show them the shirt because they don't have a green Beckenbauer jersey from the 1974 World Cup. I think they want to exhibit it for a while.

"I will never forget that match in Hamburg and the occasion, even though we lost 3-0."

You guys had to introduce yourselves to the current Socceroos in a recent official get-together. Do you feel your achievements have not been adequately recognised?

"Of course. Every time you look at an international game from overseas in Germany, Netherlands or England you can always see retired heroes doing something for the game.

"They are involved in different sorts of things, not just watching the game, so they will always be famous and popular within their own country.

"Now tell me, how would a 20-year-old Australian football fan know who I am?

"Even my grandkids at first did not even know I played for Australia and they only believed me when I showed them some little video clips."

What was coach Rasic like? What was his favourite kind of player and what was his pet hate?

"We had plenty of barneys with Rale but he always won. If you were to look at football today he would be a sort of Jose Mourinho, somebody you knew was the chief by just looking at him.

"He loved us to have a joke but at training and in games it was different. You had to do the right thing.

"We had different players come and go but Rasic always told us, 'I don't look at the player but the man'. He obviously meant that he wanted players who were capable of fitting in with us.

"Nowadays you hear things about players wanting their own room, wanting this and wanting that. Not with Rale, no chance: you had to be part of the whole group, the family.

"Today you get all these players listening to music with headphones and not even talking to each other. Rale had us as one big family in the bus, joking, singing and going mad at each other. He loved the camaraderie. He really did.

"His pet hate: he had a million of them. He used to get frustrated by players who did not give 100 per cent. He sometimes told me, 'As soon as you score a couple you switch off' and he would sub me. He was big on discipline. Without it we would never have reached the World Cup."

What are your recollections from your stint in the English first division?

"I started quite well in the first few games in 1974 when the weather was fine and I had a good match at Highbury against Arsenal when I scored and hit the post ... that's when people started taking an interest in me.

"But when the winter set in the heavy grounds became my undoing. Our home ground was often like a bog. It was like playing in mud so my game of running with the ball and taking people on went out the window. I also got injured.

"It was a difficult season and Luton ran into financial problems and could not pay me. So that's when I signed for Cardiff who agreed to pay me the money I was owed. I had a lovely time in Wales.

"Playing in the big grounds was wonderful but nothing beats the World Cup."

Which was the greatest Socceroos team?

"In my opinion if we had been full-time professionals like they are now we would have held our own with any Socceroos side.

"By that I mean same training, same conditions and same travel arrangements.

"I think the 1974 team was the best balanced of all. We were quite strong all over the field. Some other Socceroos teams had five or six good players and other ordinary ones while we were the best balanced."

Do you wish you played today?

"If you asked me if I could play today I'd say all I can hope for is a spot on the bench. The reason is I'm 68!

"Seriously, the only reason I would want to play now is the financial one.

"From a playing perspective it would have been much easier for me as a striker because there is no tackling from behind today.

"They used to follow through with the tackling and you got wiped all the time. It would've been easier and more comfortable to be able to receive the ball and bring it down. It was accepted to go for the leg and the ball at the time. Life is much better for the strikers nowadays."

Who were the best footballers you played with and against?

"Abonyi, who today would be a No 10, is the finest player I have played with by a million miles. We had a telepathic understanding of what each one of us was going to do at our club St George and with the Socceroos.

"I played against Pele and George Best but Beckenbauer would have to be the greatest I've ever played against without doubt."

* * *

'QUOTE UNQUOTE'

Sharpshooting Frank Farina was never one to take a backward step when expressing his opinion and he had some strong words of advice for the A-League.

Farina urges clubs to forget about faded stars
30 December 2019

Former Socceroos striker and coach Frank Farina believes the A-League should end its flirtation with fading superstar imports and put every effort into engaging middle-of-the-range stars who are still at their peak.

Farina, who played for Australia for more than a decade and coached the green and gold for six years, said a top playmaker like Milos Ninkovic or Thomas Broich is more likely to leave a legacy in Australia than a superstar such as Alessandro Del Piero, who is past his peak.

Farina was Sydney FC coach when the Italian FIFA World Cup winner spent the last two years of his career in Australia.

He said the short-term benefits of signing such big names as ADP are huge but in the long run but clubs' interests are better served by less talented and fitter marquees.

"Alessandro was a great player and a fantastic guy. He was a dream for the league because he created a lot of interest," Farina said.

"In terms of football it was a bit hard for him because he was not in his prime, his fitness was not at the peak and the A-League was transforming itself into a tough competition when he came here.

"He had lost his legs a little bit but he still had a charisma about him and if you gave him the ball 30 metres from goal he would do something. He did reasonably well here.

"However, I believe that in the long term you are better off getting guys like Ninkovic or Broich who were not household names when they came to Australia but look at the service they have provided."

Farina, who is one of the most respected figures in Australian football, was happy to talk about his long career that took him to the four corners of the world as a player and a coach.

You started playing in far north Queensland, which is not really known as a football heartland. You must have been pretty good to be noticed.

"You're right. North Queensland was a backwater in terms of football. I'd moved from Papua New Guinea to Australia in 1975 and played football even though it was not very big. After a while I was invited to Brisbane just when the Australian Institute of Sport was launched. I won a scholarship to go to Canberra and that's where it all started for me."

You broke several scoring records in your first stint in the NSL. Your two seasons at Marconi where you were twice best player and top scorer must still be close to your heart.

"Of course, I was young and coming through and as a striker I have great memories. I take great pride in the fact that the team won the 1988 grand final against Sydney Croatia (now Sydney United 58)."

How did the big move to FC Brugge in 1988 come about?

"Prior to the 1988 Olympics in Korea an Israeli agent was following me during two qualifiers against Israel. After the Games he made contact again and offered me a trial with Brugge.

"At that time I was a bit fed up with trials but he assured me it was more than that so I went to Belgium in October. I missed their pre-season but after a short spell they offered me a contract during a transfer window so I had a bit of luck."

Brugge won the championship in 1990 thanks largely to your 24 goals that gave you the best foreigner award. Was that the highlight of your career in Europe?

"It was an accolade for the team. It was a very difficult season and we did not hit our straps before 10 games or so. After we got knocked out of Europe and the Belgian Cup our only focus was the league and we went on an unbeaten run of about 30 games, including 10 in the following season. Again, they were great memories."

Your transfer to Bari in 1990 would become a classic case of going from the sublime to the ridiculous. What happened there?

"I went from a top club in Belgium where you had plenty of scoring opportunities to a struggling club and as a striker that becomes very difficult. It was not the best time, to be honest."

So your stint in the French league would have lifted your spirits, right?

"I got injured days before Strasbourg's first league game and I struggled at first. But it was a good league and I had a good time there."

Your appointment as player/coach with Brisbane Strikers would become the stuff of legend. Tell us about that glorious afternoon at Suncorp in 1997.

"I was just a player when I came back to Australia in 1995 and Brisbane made the finals that year for the first time. We had a pretty strong side in 1997 yet we were the underdogs for the season decider. However, it all came together against Sydney United. We performed and deservedly won 2-0 in front of a sellout crowd."

You played 37 full internationals mostly under Frank Arok and Eddie Thomson. What were they like as coaches?

"Their styles were different but both were successful. They were legends of Australian football, if you like. I had my ups and downs with each of them but I respect them highly. I had a great time in a very different era when World Cup qualifying rounds were very different. It is just unfortunate that we never managed to qualify when they were in charge."

You took part in three failed Socceroos' attempts to reach the World Cup. Which one of the defeats against Scotland in 1985, Israel in 1989 or Argentina in 1993 hurt most?

"Scotland were always going to be hard. We fell 2-0 in Glasgow and probably should have lost by more but by the same token we should have gone beyond the 0-0 draw in the return in Melbourne.

"I would say the failed campaign to reach Italia '90 was the hardest to take because we ruined everything by losing in New Zealand, a result that put us behind the eight ball. The consequence of that defeat was that we had to beat Israel in our last game at home to qualify but could only draw 1-1 so we were out. Had we beaten New Zealand the draw would have been enough.

"We went close against Argentina but the narrow 2-1 aggregate defeat did not hurt as much as the debacle from four years earlier."

Your most memorable moment in a green and gold jersey must have come at the 1988 Olympics when you scored the winning goal in a shock 1-0 win over Yugoslavia. Would that be right?

"It was up there. To be honest I mis-hit the shot that gave us victory. Alan Davidson played the ball over the top and it kept bouncing and I meant to put it to the goalkeeper's right but I mis-hit it and it went to the far post.

"For me the highlight was eliminating New Zealand in the final qualifiers to get to the '88 Olympics. We were 1-0 down in Wellington and I came off the bench to score the equaliser. A defeat in a round-robin that included Israel and Taiwan could have crushed our Olympic dream so that moment sticks out in my mind."

You also took charge of the Socceroos for six years. How close were Australia to beating Uruguay in 2001?

"We were much closer than many people would imagine. They would see the scoreline of the return which we lost 3-0 (3-1 on aggregate) but we had big opportunities when we were two down and had we scored we would have made it 2-1 and probably gone to the World Cup on away goals."

Several pundits considered you rather lucky to retain the job after that heavy defeat in Montevideo. Were you treated fairly by the media?

"I can't complain about the way I was treated. The media has a job to do and you have to respect that. And that's the way it was. I was fortunate to keep my job despite the turmoil the game was going through at the higher level at the time. Looking back, I had a great time although I must say my stint as national coach was a bit too long."

You had the privilege of working with much-loved strikers Mark Viduka and Harry Kewell. How good were they?

"The highest compliment I could possibly pay to both of them and others too is they could have played with any club and in any competition in the world. It's a big rap but nobody can tell me that 'Dukes' or 'H' could not play for AC Milan, Juventus, Barcelona or Real Madrid. They would have been at home with those teams. They were that good at that particular time in their careers."

Was it hard to 'manage' the two superstars and all the outside influences associated with their status?

"Managing them per se was not hard. They were a treat to deal with. Managing the situations that the World Cup qualification process created was the difficult part. Australia was not involved in Asia at that time so we did not have any meaningful matches in our campaigns to reach the World Cup except the last hurdle.

"Getting our best players to come over to play against Solomon Islands, Vanuatu or Fiji—countries we would beat with our second team—always created problems with their clubs because our expectation was that we should always have our strongest team and I agreed. But the bottom line is that all the players who came over did so because they wanted to play for Australia."

Any regrets in your coaching career?

"Not really because I always did it my way which sometimes got me a job and on other times the sack. But I was always easy with myself because if I were successful it was because I did things the way I wanted. At the end of the day I was always able to look at the mirror and say to myself, 'I did it my way and I don't give a rat's what others say'. I was never one to be told what to do.

"When I was with the Socceroos I was often urged to do this or pick this player but I never listened really and whether that cost me my job at the end I don't know."

Finally, who are the best players you have played with and against?

"I played with some great Australian players like Charlie Yankos, John Kosmina, David Mitchell, Graham Arnold, Jimmy Patikas, Robbie Slater, Rod Brown and Alan Hunter who were players who made a difference. Abroad I had the privilege to play alongside Belgian captain Jan Ceulemans, England's David Platt and others.

"The finest players I faced were Zinedine Zidane with whom I crossed paths when he was at Bordeaux, Argentina's Diego Maradona, Brazil's Zico and the three Dutchmen Frank Rijkaard, Marco Van Basten and Ruud Gullit."

* * *

'QUOTE UNQUOTE'

Striker Mark Viduka went on a nostalgic trip down memory lane and recalled his finest game in Europe ... and, contrary to popular belief, it wasn't his four-goal blitz against Liverpool.

The night Viduka conquered Rome
21 August 2020

Australia's 2006 World Cup captain Mark Viduka, the big striker they called the 'V-Bomber', will always be remembered universally for his four-goal demolition job on Liverpool when he was playing for Leeds United.

In his first season in Yorkshire, Viduka stole the show in a Premier League match in November 2000 which Leeds won 4-3.

Viduka's extraordinary achievement boosted his reputation as a prolific predator and instantly made him a marked man in the league and in Europe.

Many fans still regard his dazzling display on a sunny afternoon at Elland Road as the highlight of his club career.

The man himself does not see it that way, however.

"I don't like it when people suggest that was my career highlight ... simply because it was not," Viduka said from his family home in Zagreb.

"How do you define 'highlight', anyway? Winning my first league title with Melbourne Knights was a highlight and playing in a Champions League semi-final with Leeds was huge too.

"Okay, I scored four that day but I don't think it was the greatest game I ever played, to be honest. I played better games.

"For me, my best game was when we beat Lazio 1-0 in Rome in the Champions League in 2000 and I set up Alan Smith with a back-heel. I felt confident, I was taking on players and I was dangerous all night.

"I did not score at the Olimpico but that's how it is in football. Sometimes you have a great game and fail to find the net; on other occasions you have an average game, you get a couple of sniffs and you score twice."

Viduka's four goals against Liverpool made headlines around the world and even provided two women with a special thrill.

"Our manager David O'Leary is a Catholic and his mother, who was watching the game on television, was so excited when I made the sign of the cross after two of the goals I scored that she texted David straight after the match to tell him she was over the moon about me.

"That day was also my mum's birthday and she was the person I was waving and blowing kisses to at the cameras. I knew she was watching."

Viduka, who is now 44, was happy to relive some of the most important moments of his stellar career.

What has become of Viduka the footballer?

"My wife Ivana and I have a coffee shop outside Zagreb which she runs while I am getting into real estate. I just have coffees there, that's just about it."

You were raised by a club that has produced several top Socceroos. What do the Melbourne Knights mean to the city's Croatian community?

"When I was growing up in Melbourne times were different. Croatia was just a state in communist Yugoslavia then and Croats were not even allowed to say they were for a free independent nation. The immigrants who went to Australia then set up clubs like Melbourne and Sydney Croatia where they could get together and enjoy football, which is what they all had in common.

"We were all hoping that one day Croatia would be a free country and that is why through football there was so much passion at those clubs."

What made the Knights team that won the league and cup double in 1995 so special?

"We were a young squad and had got close to winning the title a couple of times but in my second-last year coach Mirko Bazic came in and made a lot of changes. It was a gamble in a way but we became a strong group on and off the pitch and it showed in my last season when we won the double. We had a quality team that comprised several Socceroos like Steve Horvat, Joe Spiteri, Tom Pondeljak and Andrew Marth."

You were always destined to end up abroad and when Croatia's first president Franjo Tudjman, on a visit to Australia in 1995, urged you to join Dinamo Zagreb you could not possibly reject him, could you?

"I was a young boy and very inexperienced. The year before I had an offer from Borussia Dortmund. I had a contract and everything and out of the blue and in the last minute Tudjman came into the picture and gave me this big speech about how he wanted me to go to Croatia to play for Dinamo.

"My whole family were excited to take a phone call from Tudjman, who invited us to have lunch with him. It was very difficult to say 'no'."

You helped Dinamo win three championships yet some fans saw you not only as a footballer but also as Tudjman's boy. Were you becoming a political tool?

"To be honest, Tudjman was setting up a new country from scratch and everything he did was designed to promote Croatia abroad. In hindsight, I think the motive behind his attempt to bring me to Croatia was to show those Croats who had left the country for political or economic reasons that it was okay to come back home so they could help build the country.

"Later on when he was getting rather unpopular, things started to affect my relationship with the fans. For example, one day I scored against Hajduk in a league match in Split and the travelling fans started booing me. It was then that I realised that football was turning into something else. I was there to play football and was not interested in politics."

Your big move to Celtic made Britain and Europe take notice of your ability. Was Parkhead a football 'paradise' for you?

"It was. Playing for Celtic was paradise in a footballing sense after what was happening to me during the latter stages of my stay in Zagreb. In Glasgow, I found genuine love for the club where we would get 60,000 fans for all matches, even those cup games against second or third division teams. Celtic's support is unbelievable. I have never seen anything like it."

You probably reached your peak during your four-year stint with Leeds. How big was O'Leary's influence on your career?

"David bought me from Celtic in 2000 for something like six million pounds and I loved playing under him. I had no complaints. He was tough when he needed to be and if you needed an arm around your shoulder, he would be there for you. He became rather unpopular with some of the players later on but I had no such experience with him. He was a great manager and I was very surprised when he got the sack for finishing fifth."

In 2001, Leeds were one match away from the Champions League final but fell to Gaizka Mendieta's Valencia. Were they too strong?

"I think so, in the end. We drew the first leg 0-0 and it became very difficult in the return in Valencia. We faced a big and vocal crowd at the Mestalla and, mind you, they had a top-quality side too. We lost 3-0. At times you have to acknowledge you are second best ... the result said it all."

For a period you and Harry Kewell were among the deadliest strikers in Europe ... different characters, different players but always on the same wavelength, on the pitch anyway.

"Definitely. I loved playing with Harry. We trained and played together for a long time and we had a really good understanding. He is one of the greatest players I have played with. He is top class."

Your transfer from Leeds to Middlesbrough in 2004 left a bad taste among some fans who might have expected you to stick around.

"I don't think so. Let me tell you something. In my football life, whenever I left a club—except for Melbourne Knights—there was always a bad feeling. I was league top scorer and players' player of the year at Celtic and when I left ... bad taste. When Henrik Larsson left Celtic and returned there with Barcelona, he was booed. And he was a legend. What does that tell you? Fans are attached to their club and usually don't like players leaving. I understand that."

The Socceroos' World Cup playoffs with Uruguay in 2001 and 2005 provided us all with wildly contrasting emotions. How did you see the two ties from the thick of the action?

"The thing is—up until we got into Asia in 2006—we used to play easy matches in Oceania and had to perform in two matches against some South American team that would have gone through a whole series of tough qualifiers in their region. This gave the South Americans a massive advantage, as if they were not already strong enough in their own right.

"The two ties had different scenarios and were both very close. I think the second time around under Guus Hiddink we were better organised, especially in defence. Sometimes it's the little details or a bit of luck that can get you over the line. When we got through via a shootout in Sydney in 2005, the tie could have gone either way."

What went through your mind when you missed your penalty in the tense shootout with so much on the line?

"At that moment I was devastated but Mark Schwarzer saved us with two great stops. That miss cost me a few beers and coffees."

You would have felt very proud and privileged to lead Australia in their first World Cup in 32 years in 2006.

"I was very proud of course and, having grown up with many of my teammates, I was happy for our generation to be able to get a chance to play in the World Cup."

Was the Italy game in Kaiserslautern a missed opportunity? Should the Socceroos have had a real go at them?

"It's difficult to say. I thought Italy played really well that day and they went on to win the World Cup after getting through some big games. Hindsight is a wonderful thing and, as they say, everybody is a general after the battle. At the time I thought Hiddink would bring on John Aloisi earlier when the Italians had Marco Materazzi sent off, but perhaps he was saving his cards for extra time. Who was to know they would get a penalty in the last moments?"

You were an excellent target man for Australia. Is that role one of football's thankless jobs?

"Look, sometimes it is, sometimes it isn't. For Australia, I usually played as a lone striker but I preferred the two-striker system I played in at club level. I was never a fast player and I always preferred another striker near me because it is hard to make headway as a main striker if the wingers are too far apart.

"I'll explain. If I'm playing as a lone striker and facing two defenders, one of them can mark me and take chances because he's not scared since he knows there is another defender covering him. If on the other hand I am one of two strikers facing two defenders, I can keep them on their toes and neither would be keen to commit too much because if one of them does and I turn I'm away and he's on the turf. I am sure most strikers would prefer to play in a two-pronged attack."

Who was the toughest defender you played against?

"When we played against Valencia in the Champions League semis I found stopper Roberto Ayala an incredibly hard defender to deal with. He was not very tall but very clever and very strong."

When you retired 11 years ago, you kept a very low profile when many expected you to try your hand at coaching. It appears the dugout is not for you.

"Whether it is for me or not I wouldn't know because I have never tried it. After I quit, I consciously wanted to spend more time with my family and see our three sons grow up after I dedicated so many years of my life to football. When you are a professional player, everything revolves around football ... winning, losing, moving from one club to another and so on. I had been in the spotlight and under pressure from a very young age and it obviously was very stressful and it takes it out of you."

Finally, who were the best players you have played with and against?

"Kewell no doubt was my best teammate at club and Socceroos level. I should also mention Frenchman Olivier Dacourt who was an incredible midfielder at Leeds.

"The best player I faced at international level would have to be midfielder Zinedine Zidane. We played the French in Melbourne in 2001 and he was amazing. He is top, top class. At club level, as I said, Ayala stands out."

* * *

Mark Bresciano had a career most children can only dream of but when he started dreading the game, he knew it was time to hang up his boots.

The day Bresciano knew it was time to quit
14 February 2017

Australia's World Cup midfielder Mark Bresciano revealed he did not fulfil his dream of ending his career back home simply because he became sick of the game he loved and adorned for many years.

Bresciano, one of the true gentlemen of Australian sport, said he would have loved to give something back to the game that launched his successful career, but he just could not do it as a professional anymore and did not want to do the wrong thing by whichever club engaged him.

"There were times when I was keen to come back to Australia and play in the A-League," Bresciano said.

"Honestly, my intentions were to come back after my contract was up in Qatar.

"But I didn't think I would finish my career this early.

"I remember one day I was driving to training in Qatar and it just hit me that I wanted to head back and go home and not go to training any more.

"That day was when I made the decision: 'That's it, I'm done, I'm finished and I don't want to do this anymore'.

"I did not want to come back to Australia half-hearted and with less than a 100 per cent commitment. I would have preferred to continue playing but I just couldn't do it.

"I could not commit. I had had enough and I needed a break."

Bresciano said he fully understood the sentiments of fellow Socceroos star Mark Schwarzer who once said that national team stars had a lot to lose by coming back to Australia because of the tall poppy syndrome that unfortunately is part of our football culture.

"I know where he was coming from, but this is not the reason I did not come back," he said.

"Schwarzer had a marvellous career and had he returned home, he would have done so towards the end of his playing time, well past his peak.

"People judge you on the last game you play and there have been instances of former Socceroos stars like John Aloisi, Harry Kewell and Vince Grella coming back and being under intense scrutiny.

"But again, I did not think of this when I decided to quit the game."

Bresciano, who turned 37 at the weekend, lives in his home town Melbourne. He spoke at length about his professional career that spanned 16 years.

So what are you doing now?

"I'm still not involved in football at the moment. Before I came home I went to Italy for six months to do a sports director's course in Florence.

"Not that I got any opportunities but mentally I am not ready to get back into the game so I occupy myself now doing some little projects and developments in Melbourne."

You've had a long and illustrious career. If you were not such a fine footballer what career path would you have taken?

"I was studying to be some sort of engineer. My family is in the building game so I guess I would have followed their path if football did not get into my way."

Serie A was very good to you ... and you were pretty good to Empoli, Parma, Palermo and Lazio, mind you. What did Italian football teach you?

"The lesson you learn in Italy does not relate to just football. It also gives you a strong education in general life, it teaches you to respect people and makes you work hard and keep fighting to earn your stripes, same as in other decent league in Europe."

You must have some great stories to tell. What was the highlight of your stint in Italy?

"I will never forget my first three years in Italy at Empoli, first because we got promoted to Serie A and also because I was playing alongside one of my best mates Grella. We had a great time and we enjoyed our football back then.

"I'm not saying that I did not enjoy myself at other clubs but your first experience in a new country is always special."

Your stay in Italy also left you with the bad memory of a riot that broke out outside the stadium during a Catania versus Palermo match in 2007. What do you remember from that day that saw a policeman killed and dozens of fans injured?

"I was a Palermo player then. It was my worst experience in Italy, one hundred per cent. I was devastated and it was probably the time I decided to leave Italy. I could not play there anymore after seeing something like that.

"It had nothing to do with the game and it pushed you away from it.

"The people in Italy are very fanatical, but you can almost always expect some 'complications' in games."

Soon after that incident you were on the verge of joining Manchester City but somehow the deal fell through at the last minute. What happened?

"The deal was done and I had already signed my personal contract. I had started training in Manchester and was house-hunting and getting ready for the first game of 2007–08.

"City manager Sven-Goran Eriksson even phoned me at three in the morning to tell me that everything was sorted.

"But there was a problem with the transfer fee and when I went back to Palermo to finalise everything I was told that there was no deal. The club president pulled the pin and decided he did not want to sell anymore and told me I would remain a Palermo player.

"I was shocked. I wanted out of the place. It was one of the worst moments of my career.

"I went on to play two more seasons for Palermo."

Correct me if I'm wrong: one of your finest skills was your ability to put your body between the ball and the opponent. Was this something you learned in Italy?

"Funny you say that. It's a simple part of football. I learned that skill at the Australian Institute of Sport in Canberra. They always made us focus on that aspect, especially us midfielders."

How best would you define yourself: a pure playmaker or an attacking midfielder?

"You know what, in the early stages of my career I was an attacking midfielder because I was a lot more explosive and agile. Towards the end of my playing time, I had become a lot smarter but it is human nature that I also became slower so I gradually turned into a playmaker."

You will always be remembered as an exemplary professional who was always in control of his temperament. Did you ever lose it or get sent off?

"I can't remember being sent off or getting two yellow cards in one game. I probably got into trouble with the refs once or twice when I was at Palermo, probably due to the frustration I was feeling after my transfer to Man City did not get through.

"I tried never to lose it on the field because if you do that, you lose a lot of energy. I know it is very hard for some (players) to stay in control, but I always tried to check my feelings."

Many of your Socceroos colleagues regard the victory over Uruguay in Sydney in 2005 as the finest moment of their international career. Was it yours as well?

"I think I would have to agree. It was the first time we had qualified in 32 years. It was a very special moment also because most of us would become close mates."

Your 'statue' goal celebration became famous. How could you show so little emotion after you levelled the tie against Uruguay while the whole place was going berserk? For goodness' sake, you were not playing Fiji in a friendly!

"It probably showed the level of control I have in a game. People have asked me, 'How do you score such a vital goal and not go crazy?' When the ball hit the back of the net I just froze.

"You probably did not see much of me from the outside but, believe me, on the inside there were fireworks going on. I was on fire."

You took part in three World Cups under different coaches: can you describe briefly how Guus Hiddink, Pim Verbeek and Ange Postecoglou operated?

"Hiddink knew exactly what he wanted and did it his own way. He was also capable of bringing the best out of every player.

"Verbeek was not so much soft, but he was a bit more lenient towards certain players and was incapable of getting the best out of some players in the team.

"Regarding Postecoglou, I have never met a coach who is as ambitious as Ange. He was a great dreamer and he talked to us the same way he talked to the media.

"He had nothing to hide and let everyone know of his intentions. He dreamed and he tried everything possible to make it possible. And I think he's getting his rewards."

So who was the best coach you have worked with at club or national level?

"As I said before, a lot of my early education came from the AIS and Steve O'Connor taught me all the basics but then as you get experienced and play in the big leagues you come across some top coaches.

"Cesare Prandelli was very good for me at Parma and so was Francesco Guidolin at Palermo."

What do you think of the current Socceroos team? What are their strengths and weaknesses?

"The positive and attacking style that Ange has introduced is the team's main strength. The Socceroos' game depends on possession, intensity and creative football that provides the team with scoring opportunities.

"On the other side of the ledger I sometimes think that our defenders are not in the best position to counter the opposition's attack and are torn open.

"Today many people believe that attacks start from the back but sometimes they forget that defenders are there essentially to defend."

The Socceroos are Asian champions and should make their fourth straight FIFA World Cup while the A-League is still going strong after 12 difficult years. Do you reckon that many people still do not believe in Australian football?

"I think the Socceroos and the A-League are different in regard to their appeal. From what I see now, people do believe in the A-League when you consider the number of people who go to the games and watch it on television. So I think it is well supported.

"When it comes to the national team, the only people who have negative vibes are those from the older generation. Maybe this is a result of how much disappointment we have had in the past, those years of not making the World Cup.

"But the new generation has embraced the game at several levels."

Finally, two standard questions: Who were the best players you have played with and against?

"Italy defender Fabio Cannavaro stands out for me. I had the privilege of playing with him at Parma and I will never forget the way he trained and played. He was the ultimate professional and he treated any training session like a World Cup final. He was an all-round good player.

"The best player I faced was Brazilian midfielder Emerson. I was at Parma and I remember a game we played against Roma in Serie A and at the end of the match I said to myself, 'I had no chance with this guy'. He was so skilful."

And who are the players you admire most in Australia and abroad?

"One player in the A-League who has caught my eye is Melbourne City midfielder Luke Brattan. I watched him play a couple of games and this kid can play. I also like Celtic's Tom Rogic, who is a player with special skills other players don't have and his confidence is growing.

"Overseas it has got to be Lionel Messi. I am a spectator now and I just love watching him play. He has some unbelievable skills but the way he plays he makes things look so easy."

The Obituaries

They are the football stories that are never easy to write yet obituaries provide a platform for a meaningful appreciation of the careers and lives of those who had left a mark on the game.

The news of Les Murray's death in July 2017 came as a shock to many of his friends and admirers. I felt I should pen a few words in appreciation of his friendship.

Les Murray made Australia love the world game
31 July 2017

In late 2004 I phoned Laszlo for a huge favour, one of many he would do for me in the course of our 36-year friendship.

I was looking after the football coverage of Sydney's *The Daily Telegraph* in those days and on the morning of November 7 we had an unpleasant story to report: Johnny Warren had lost his battle with cancer.

The sports editor wanted a fitting obituary. There's no other person, I told him: it's got to be Les Murray.

I rang Les in the early afternoon to ask him for a tribute to one of his best mates.

He had had a couple of drinks to drown his sorrows but he said: "Of course, Philip, when do you want it?"

"Now," I replied.

As always, Les did not fail me and in an hour or so he filed a beautifully crafted and heartfelt obituary on his old friend and collaborator and the Tele gave it the prominence it richly deserved.

Les was that sort of bloke: loyal to his friends, generous with his time and always there when you needed him.

He just could not say 'no' to anyone.

One day I rang him for a quote on a breaking story and he sounded a bit tired.

He still gave me the quote, mind you, even though it was in the middle of the night in Mongolia.

Les, who died on Monday after a long illness aged 71, was a man of style and he loved life because he was a citizen of the world which for him had no borders.

He needed his comforts and his top hotels to be sure and in his many travels he would always seek a good meal and an even better red to round off the day.

But the flashy and glitzy restaurants were never really his preferred option. "Let's find a typical place with character where the locals go," he once told me.

This is because if he happened to be in Indonesia, South Africa, Bolivia or Uzbekistan he reckoned the best way to learn about a country and its culture is to mix with the locals in a place that looked and felt like their own, not one belonging to some multinational chain.

It's called respect, which is probably why he always made an effort to learn the right pronunciation of every first and second name he uttered either on television or in private conversation.

If you are going to mention anyone you owe it to him or her to pronounce the name correctly, he would say.

Modern Aussie journalism could do very nicely with such high standards.

Australian football is reeling from the passing of a true icon of the world game, whose impeccable behaviour, real football mentality and high standing in the community will not be forgotten easily.

When I came to Australia in 1981 and soon discovered to my deep frustration the game's place in a country besotted with such strange games as Australian Rules, rugby league and cricket, Les would offer solace and plenty of conversations about the game we both loved with a passion.

He would probably have been the only one I talked to who knew that the European Cup was not some sort of foreign gelato to hit our stores but football's most important club competition.

He knew that there was more to foreign football than Liverpool, Manchester United and the FA Cup.

And he knew above all that if Australia was to make it in the world game it would have to learn to appreciate the value and appeal of football at large.

Les was generous enough to introduce me to SBS and I will always be grateful for that.

He leaves us with a rich legacy and a massive hole to fill.

The game is much stronger now than it was when he made his first tentative steps in Australia in the late 1970s.

It enjoys a profile that he has helped build with his sheer professionalism, dedication and love for the game.

Yet the greatest legacy he could leave is for aspiring journalists to follow in his footsteps and learn to report with fairness and respect and without fear.

Les Murray led by example throughout his career and I'm sure he will keep fighting for our game deep into extra time.

* * *

Socceroos coach Pim Verbeek sparked controversy by his unflattering appraisal of the A-League yet when he lost his battle with cancer many were sad to see a fine gentleman go.

Verbeek was a victim of our delusions of grandeur
29 November 2019

Former Socceroos coach Pim Verbeek, who has lost his battle with cancer aged 63, sadly will be remembered for an infamous quote that immediately put him offside with many within Australia's football fraternity.

The Dutchman took up the national team job in late 2007 and led the Socceroos to their second straight FIFA World Cup before leaving the position after South Africa 2010.

Many people were glad to see him go because they saw in him the quintessential football pragmatist who only cared about one thing: results.

The Socceroos had little trouble qualifying for the World Cup finals but in South Africa a big shock awaited them.

'Pimbecile' screamed a Sydney newspaper after a World Cup 4-0 drubbing in their first match against Germany in Durban.

The Socceroos would be eliminated at the group stage but they exited the tournament with an impressive 2-1 victory over Serbia.

Yet it was his appraisal of the A-League's quality early in his tenure that unfortunately might have sealed his legacy.

In a press conference in Sydney to announce his first squad he was asked why Michael Beauchamp and Josh Kennedy were selected when they were getting very little game time with their respective German second division clubs Nurnberg and Karlsruhe.

Verbeek replied bluntly: "If you train for three weeks with Nurnberg or Karlsruhe,

I have to be honest, I still think that's better than playing in the A-League."

That comment, which of course was spot on, did not go down well with all those who thought the world of Australian football after the relative success of the Socceroos in the 2006 World Cup and the formation of the professional A-League.

How dare he speaks so unkindly of our top competition, asked many pundits who had lost all sense of proportion and perspective in a classic case of delusions of grandeur.

Yet the very people who may have seen Verbeek as an arrogant pragmatist who had the temerity to speak his mind and tell it the way it is conveniently overlooked the fact that he was a thorough professional who loved his job with a passion ... and was pretty good at it, too.

He was without doubt one of the most pleasant coaches and genuine persons I have had the pleasure to deal with.

He was a true gentleman in a murky football world full of suspicion, selfishness and subterfuge.

He was a deep thinker who left nothing to chance when it came to preparing for a football match.

"That's my job. I'm thinking all the time when I'm in camp of how's the best way to win a match," he once told me.

"But sometimes in away games it is just not worth taking the risk with attack."

Verbeek's meticulous approach came across clearly on the occasion of a World Cup qualifier against Uzbekistan in Tashkent in 2009.

On the eve of the match, he spoke about his plan to play it cautiously in the first 20 minutes or so in the hope of making the impatient Uzbek fans get on their team's back and force them to play into Australia's hands by taking a few risks.

He later came up to me and asked me to leave out the bit about the home fans in my preview because his quotes could be picked up by the Uzbek media and spark an unnecessary hostile reaction at the ground.

"I do not want to give the Uzbeks the chance to say, 'Okay, if that's what he wants'," he explained. Australia would win 1-0.

That was Pim Verbeek to a tee. A top coach and a great man who deserved better recognition in Australia.

* * *

'QUOTE UNQUOTE'

Diego Maradona, who died of a heart attack at the age 60, will always be remembered for four extraordinary minutes at the 1986 World Cup that sealed his legacy.

Maradona the epitome of a flawed genius
26 November 2020

Diego Maradona, who died of a heart attack at the age of 60, will always be remembered for four extraordinary minutes at the 1986 World Cup that sealed his legacy.

And the massive popularity he enjoyed due to his extraordinary exploits on the football fields of the world is best illustrated by the moving condolences expressed by dozens of football personalities and the outpouring of grief in the two countries he touched by his brilliance: Argentina and Italy.

Maradona was an inspirational captain but also a flawed genius, no doubt about that.

His sublime skill as an attacking footballer and his ability to lead by example enabled an average Argentina side to win the 1986 FIFA World Cup.

Mexico '86 was Maradona's tournament same as Mexico '70 was Pele's and France '98 was Zinedine Zidane's.

At club level Maradona turned battling Napoli into Serie A giants and played a key role in the club's two championships in 1987 and 1990.

Michel Platini, who crossed paths with him many times in the 1980s, once said that "what Zidane could do with a ball Maradona could do with an orange".

Yet controversy and Maradona were never mutually exclusive.

On his way to leading the 'Albiceleste' to global glory in the land of the Aztecs, Maradona's legacy would be established in four memorable minutes that stunned the world.

In a tense quarter-final against England in Mexico City, the Argentine broke the deadlock after 51 minutes with an illegal strike that would become known as the 'Hand of God' goal.

Vying for a high ball with goalkeeper Peter Shilton, Maradona knew the only way he could beat the much taller opponent was by using his hands and that is what he did ... he punched the ball home, ran away to celebrate and got away with it.

It was not the first time someone had tried to break the rules to seek an unfair advantage and it would not be the last.

But what angered the English was the way he seemed to be taking the mickey out of the beaten team by invoking the hand of God and justified his action by claiming 'revenge' for the Falklands war Argentina had lost to Britain four years earlier.

Not long after reaching the bottom of football integrity, however, Maradona scaled the heights of the game's immortality when he picked up the ball in his own half and went on to beat half the England team in a mazy run before planting the ball in Shilton's net for one of the greatest goals ever scored.

The Argentine was at the peak of his mesmeric might in 1986 and a year later he led his club Napoli to the first championship in their history.

He was treated like a god in the southern Italian city which is probably where his off-field problems started.

Away from the spotlight, he started mixing with the wrong people—notably the local Camorra crime syndicate—but the club turned a blind eye to his indiscretions.

Napoli knew about this but were not overly concerned. Their attitude appeared to be 'as long as he delivers on the field he can do whatever he likes in his free time'.

Drug addiction rumours were becoming stronger by the week and matters come to a head in 1991 when he was suspended for 15 months for cocaine use.

It is when Maradona saw Naples and 'died'.

His stellar career was in serious turmoil yet he would come back to help his country qualify for the 1994 World Cup at the expense of Australia.

I will always cherish the one-on-one interview I had with the great man at a hotel in Sydney a few days before the first leg of the playoff with the Socceroos (see the Big Interviews section).

He lamented the excessive money in football that was putting its top players under too much pressure and complained about the lack of protection for the game's entertainers from unscrupulous defenders.

In America he was sensationally kicked out of the tournament after he failed another drug test. His troubled career as a professional footballer was effectively over.

He later would dabble with coaching with scant success.

And now that his extraordinary life has come to an end, I just hope that for all his faults and weaknesses, Diego Armando Maradona will be remembered as a magnificent footballer who enjoyed life and gave joy to hundreds of millions of fans around the world.

Muchas gracias, Diego.

* * *

'QUOTE UNQUOTE'

Italy striker Paolo Rossi became a national hero after playing a key role in the Azzurri's 1982 World Cup triumph. His sudden passing stunned the football-mad country and the rest of the world.

The three matches that defined Rossi's career
10 December 2020

The death of Italian World Cup hero Paolo Rossi has revived memories of when the ruthless striker with the angelic face gave the Azzurri one of their grandest triumphs on the global stage.

Rossi died in the early hours of Thursday morning (AEDT), RAI-TV announced.

The cause of his death is unknown. He was 64.

The man stole the hearts of millions of Italians by scoring six goals in the latter stages of the 1982 FIFA World Cup in Spain, which Italy won.

His predatory instincts also broke the hearts of millions of Brazilians after he grabbed a poacher's hat-trick to help Italy win 3–2 and knock out one of the greatest Brazil sides of all time in an all-time classic in Barcelona.

Rossi added two more goals in the semi-final against Poland which the Italians won 2–0 and he opened the scoring in the Azzurri's 3–1 win over West Germany in the final in Madrid.

His six goals that made him the leading scorer of the competition were a microcosm of the perfect striker.

From the way he lost Junior to head home his opener against Brazil, his alertness to turn almost full circle to stab home the winning goal in the same match, his ability to be in the right space at the right time to head in the clincher against Poland and his perfect timing to connect with an inswinging cross from Claudio Gentile in the final.

Italian football had a new hero to cherish although purists would suggest that 'Pablito' was a fitter and more complete footballer four years earlier when he helped Italy to fourth place in the World Cup in Argentina.

Rossi, who was a Juventus player in 1982, was a worldwide celebrity and the star attraction when the 'Bianconeri' toured Australia two years later.

Socceroos centre-half David Ratcliffe, who faced Rossi three times, said he was "very sad" to hear of the news.

"I was actually marking him in the three matches and I still have his shirt," Ratcliffe said.

"He obviously was a very good player to deal with. He had scored in the World Cup final only two years earlier. It's very sad news. So soon after Diego Maradona's death, too. This has not been a good year for football."

Yet Rossi's defining moment of his career nearly did not happen.

The striker was suspended for three years for his part in the betting scandal that rocked Calcio in 1980 while he was on the books of Perugia.

He missed the European Championships on home soil that same year and would have been ineligible for the World Cup in Spain too had his suspension not been reduced by one year.

He has always maintained his innocence.

He went into the Spanish football fiesta with just three Serie A matches under his belt and cut a forlorn figure in the first phase of the tournament in which Italy scraped into the next round with three unconvincing draws against Poland, Peru and Cameroon.

Rossi was largely ineffectual and the Italian media was calling for him to be dropped.

But manager Enzo Bearzot stuck with him in the next round-robin against Argentina and Brazil because he knew that, like most strikers, all he needed was one goal and his confidence would return.

Rossi showed signs of a revival during Italy's 2–1 win over the Argentines before he stole the limelight in the fixture with Brazil.

Bearzot's brave decision was vindicated because Rossi became the key ingredient of a richly talented side that was captained by goalkeeper Dino Zoff that just needed someone to stick the ball in the net.

Paolo Rossi was their man.

*   *   *

Socceroos coach Frank Arok was responsible for giving Australian football the belief that it could take on the world's best. His death came as a big blow to those who remember his 'mad dog' antics.

'Mad dog' Arok was a true believer
13 January 2021

The greatest contribution former Socceroos coach Frank Arok made to the Australian game was the way he changed the football family's mindset and made it believe that anything was possible with the right approach.

Arok, who coached the national team from 1983 to 1989, has died at the age of 88.

Tributes have flown since the news emerged on Tuesday evening of his passing.

Arok was not merely a football coach with a wide knowledge of the game, an eye for young talent and an ability to motivate his players to great heights.

The Yugoslav-born former journalist of Hungarian descent—his original name is Ferenc Arok—was also a football academic who rose to prominence after coaching St George in the early 1980s in the National Soccer League.

He would play a key role in establishing a winning culture across the country and removing to a degree the innate inferiority complex that surrounded the game in Australia at all levels.

He might have rubbed some people the wrong way in his pursuit of success. I remember England manager Bobby Robson lamenting Arok's defensive tactics that earned the Socceroos a 0-0 draw in a tour match at the Sydney Cricket Ground in 1983.

Arok, of course, used the three-match series with England as preparation for the 1986 FIFA World Cup campaign and wanted to show his players that they were strong enough to mix it with the best.

And by doing that he hoped that the whole football fraternity would come around to the idea that Australia should shed its mentality that accepted mediocrity and set loftier goals.

The Socceroos failed in the end to reach the promised land of Mexico after falling narrowly to Scotland in a final two-legged playoff.

Machiavellian Arok wanted to maximise home advantage and urged the Australian Soccer Federation to stage the return in steamy Darwin in a bid to make life as uncomfortable as possible for the Scots.

His request was rejected on economic grounds and after Alex Ferguson's side won 2-0 on a freezing night at Hampden they travelled to Melbourne where they held out for a goalless draw that gave them a ticket to the finals.

Arok's crowning glory for the Socceroos would come in 1988 when he masterminded two of the Socceroos' finest ever victories.

In a Bicentennial Gold Cup group match against Argentina in June, the Socceroos played above themselves to thrash the world champions 4-1 in Sydney.

It was an occasion that was immortalised by Charlie Yankos's long-distance bombshell that would have gone viral had it happened in today's social media environment.

"That result made people outside the game take serious notice of the Socceroos," Arok told me when I caught up with him six years ago.

A few months later at the Seoul Olympics, Australia caused a sensation when they overcame Yugoslavia 1-0 to reach the knockout stage of the competition. The winning goal came from striker Frank Farina.

Perhaps the last word on Arok's qualities as a person and a coach should go to Farina, who in 1984 earned the first of his 37 caps under the man they called 'mad dog'.

"Frank was my first Socceroos coach," said Farina, who became Australia coach from 1999 to 2005.

"He was a deep thinker and obsessed with football. I can't remember a conversation which didn't involve football.

"He told me that he wouldn't talk to me again if I didn't sign for his team St George while we were on tour with the national team in 1984. But he kept picking me for the Socceroos so I guess he forgave me.

"His legacy will continue with all the players his journey crossed, which is many."

Farina's views would resonate with anyone whose life has been touched by the mercurial Arok.

Ask anyone else who played under Arok at club or national level and he will tell you that the coach was a motivator extraordinaire, someone who would believe in you and trust you if you commit to his cause.

Do the wrong thing and you're history.

Rest in peace, Frank.

The Top Brass

Australia's football administration has had to deal with severe and justified criticism over the years for its running of the domestic game. I had my say, too.

*Brisbane Strikers and Canberra Cosmos
were the unfortunate victims of Soccer Australia's decision in 2001
to cull the struggling national league to 12 teams.*

It's time for the promotion of relegation
9 June 2001

What is it with Australian sport? Why are sporting bodies so frightened of the second division concept?

It's a term that simply does not exist in this country's sporting vernacular.

It's a stigma, a death warrant and something to avoid just like the plague.

Yet if Soccer Australia had the foresight to create such a safety net for its battling clubs, Brisbane and Canberra would not be on the scrapheap today.

Soccer Australia, with a history of spectacular bungles spanning decades, this week culled the national league to 12 teams.

In so doing, it retained clubs whose troublesome fans continue to tarnish the game's image in Australia and gave the Strikers and Cosmos a good kick in the guts.

It is hard to comprehend this latest bout of unmitigated madness.

Apart from having fewer States represented in a 'national' league, two questions must be asked.

Why is financial viability a sole criteria for acceptance in a sporting competition? And why should Soccer Australia pick and choose who plays in the league, anyway?

If Soccer Australia believes its national league should have no more than 12 teams, so be it.

But who plays in it should be determined by results on the field.

And this is where the concept of promotion and relegation comes in.

Although a second division club might discover that sponsors are much harder to find, sometimes the 'big drop' can be the best thing for a team that has lost its way.

Struggling clubs usually go down to second division purgatory—some might call it hell—until they get their act together.

If they regularly fail to get promoted they sometimes die a natural death and would have no one else to blame but themselves.

But to kill them off on the basis of a recommendation from some consulting firm does not appear to be the right way to go.

Australian soccer is basking in the glory of the national team's shock victory over France in the Confederations Cup and a thrilling league grand final between Wollongong and South Melbourne.

But as so often happens in Australian football, a feel-good moment does not last long.

Soccer Australia's head honchos saw to that this week with their folly.

There is still enough time for football's governing body to rectify its unfortunate mistake.

It should realise that promotion and relegation works well all over the world and there is no reason it cannot work here. It's worth at least a try.

Such a system would seem to be a fairer and more sensible way of solving the problems that continue to afflict the game.

But then, as we have seen over and over again, Soccer Australia is not exactly overflowing with common sense, is it?

*   *   *

The Australian game's governing body boldly decided to change its name in 2004 and the fans could not be happier.

Soccer to call itself football
9 November 2004

The Australian Soccer Association will give a red card to its little-liked name and be known as Football Australia.

The dramatic change will take place in the new year, sources said.

As a fitting and lasting tribute to former Socceroos captain Johnny Warren who lost his battle against cancer at the weekend, the domestic game's new governing body has unofficially decided to change its corporate name to Football Federation of Australia and be known thereafter as Football Australia.

There are no business, commercial or legal aspects to stop the organisation from altering its name.

The football governing body's name change and subsequent reference of the sport as 'football' is not expected to face too much opposition from rival codes like rugby league or rugby union.

But it won't go down well with the Melbourne-based Australian Football League which considers itself as the country's leading football organisation.

AFL chief executive Andrew Demetriou said yesterday it was too early to comment on the matter.

"We'll have to see what happens and then act accordingly," Demetriou said.

ASA chief executive John O'Neill refused to comment on this development that should delight thousands of round-ball fans who feel more at ease with the word 'football' than 'soccer'.

Warren, who for a quarter of a century exerted huge influence on Australian football, often voiced his opposition to the round-ball code being called 'soccer' while 95 per cent of the world called it football, futbol, fussball, futebol or whatever.

He would be pleased to know that his cherished dream is coming true.

"Wow. This will show the world that we are ready to be part of the big football family,' former Socceroos captain and midfielder Paul Wade declared.

"This must be what O'Neill meant when he said Australia was looking at the bigger picture."

* * *

Frank Lowy raised many eyebrows when he talked up his dream of an Asian super league while the A-League was still in its infancy.

Lowy's Asian dream is pure fantasy
27 August 2006

Football's head honcho Frank Lowy is the sort of person who usually gets what he wants.

But when the game's billionaire benefactor expressed his dream of a rich 'Asian Super League' last week, ordinary fans would have been perfectly entitled to wonder what was going on.

Here we are at the start of the second A-League, which could make or break football in this country, and the game's head is talking up a rebel league with rich clubs from

Japan, China and South Korea.

We've been in Asia for less than a year and already we are contemplating a rebel series—as distinct to the existing Champions League—that could divide Asian football.

How could Lowy be so elitist and misguided as to go against the 'walk before you run' principles he set out for a league that would have been on its knees without Fox's sponsorship?

And in the same breath he promised he would not undermine the league.

How could he even think about destroying in one fell swoop all the work he has done for our football?

If top league clubs from our major cities were allowed to concentrate on lucrative competition against Asian clubs, the fledgling domestic game would die instantly.

FIFA and the AFC thankfully won't allow this.

So Lowy's fantasy will always be just an idea.

A very bad one, too.

* * *

As Australia embarked on a bid to stage the World Cup, an AFC official warned that the Australians had no chance of success unless Asia presented only one bidder.

Aussies' World Cup bid is doomed, says Velappan
18 March 2009

Australia's dream of staging the World Cup is doomed to fail unless Asia comes up with a single unified bid, an influential official warned.

Former Asian confederation general secretary Peter Velappan has pleaded with the Asian Football Confederation to present one bid for the World Cup because five independent candidates is a recipe for disaster.

Australia is among five countries from the AFC that has applied to host the world's biggest sporting event in 2018 or 2022.

The others are Japan, Korea Republic, Indonesia and Qatar although the Koreans and Qataris are only interested in 2022.

"Going into the bidding process for the World Cup with five countries is suicide for Asia," Velappan said.

"It is absolutely crazy for Australia, Japan, Korea, Indonesia and Qatar to go for the same World Cup independently.

"In the current situation (of unrest within the AFC) this will have a serious backlash on our candidates.

"From my experience I can tell you it is best to send one candidate for 2018 and one for 2022.

"The AFC should gather all five candidates internally and say, okay, we put up one candidate for each of the two World Cups."

Velappan said he agreed with the Europeans who were contemplating a "preliminary" qualification process to establish one candidate so as to avoid a split vote and he thought Asia should follow the European example first mooted by UEFA president Michel Platini two months ago.

"If the Europeans think this is a good idea why can't we follow them?" he said.

"It is common sense to nominate one candidate from each continent.

"It would be a disaster to go with five separate candidates and a huge waste of time and money. England or Europe are big favourites to get 2018 but 2022 is not a guarantee either for Asia because there is the USA, too.

"If there are five Asian countries running around the world trying to win votes among FIFA's 24-member executive committee by spending millions of dollars, this is really not advisable."

Velappan, who is at loggerheads with AFC president Mohamed Bin Hammam over several issues including the latter's moves to take the governing body's headquarters away from Kuala Lumpur, said he deplored tiny Qatar's decision to muddy the waters by joining the bidding process.

"Qatar's bid is a joke," Velappan said of Bin Hammam's country.

"It has a population of 220,000 and four small stadiums. Where the hell are you holding a 32-team World Cup?"

Velappan said the Asian confederation had lost its unity since Bin Hammam took over the presidency in 2002 and it would not surprise anybody if he was voted out of his position on FIFA's executive committee and replaced by Bahrain's Sheikh Salman Ebrahim Al Khalifa, who has garnered plenty of support the last few weeks.

"We gave Bin Hammam a wonderful Asian family that included the Arabs from the west, the former Soviet republics and China, which was a difficult member for many years," Velappan said.

"But after being re-elected in 2006 he started breaking up this family with his divide-and-rule style and now he is a dictator.

"It's not about Asia or its 46 member associations anymore. It's all about him. This is not good for our football.

"Fortunately members are beginning to realise that we have a dictator in our midst.

"He was given a democratic institution and he has turned it into a desert kingdom. I am sure these issues will be considered when the AFC has its general meeting on May 8."

Efforts to contact Bin Hammam proved unsuccessful.

* * *

Football Federation Australia's draconian way of running the game angered many stakeholders and gave the A-League clubs added fuel in their fight for independence.

Faltering FFA have lost the dressing room
2 November 2015

The public relations disaster surrounding the prospect of Wellington Phoenix getting booted out of the A-League and a third Sydney team taking their place has emphasised the need for the clubs to run their own competition.

There is now too much dissatisfaction with and mistrust of Football Federation Australia's modus operandi for the 10 league clubs to keep expecting strong leadership from the governing body.

It is clear that FFA have lost the dressing room and something has to give if Australian club football is to negotiate the forthcoming years with a degree of confidence, assurance and positivity.

There is huge and widespread discontent at A-League level with the draconian way FFA deal with their clubs, whose owners have invested millions of dollars and would be perfectly entitled to walk away if they find they cannot even safeguard their own investments.

If a well-run club like Phoenix can be treated so shabbily by the FFA, every other club in the league would have every reason to feel nervous about its place at the table.

FFA will claim they always hear what the clubs have to say … but do they actually listen? Many people do not think so.

The cringeworthy spectacle of FFA chairman Frank Lowy issuing a strong statement berating Sydney FC chairman Scott Barlow and coach Graham Arnold for voicing their legitimate concerns about a third Sydney team left a bad taste.

Using the sort of language one would expect to hear at a pub, Lowy did not mince his words and made it very clear who is running the game.

Even if he was right, Lowy did not have to go public with his vitriolic attack on two men who have made a telling contribution to the A-League over the years.

The best coaches will never criticise their players in public.

Those who do are usually seen as having lost the plot.

Lowy's startling tirade came a few weeks after chief executive David Gallop forced Australia coach Ange Postecoglou to publicly back down from his well-intentioned position of neutrality regarding FFA's dispute with Professional Footballers Australia over the Collective Bargaining Agreement.

These two unfortunate episodes illustrated once again the FFA's infamous "my way or the highway" approach that has alienated many of the game's stakeholders and broken the bond of goodwill that had existed between the governing body and the clubs.

Which is why the A-League is suffering collateral damage and which is why the 10 league entities should be allowed to determine their own fortunes by setting up an executive body that is independent of FFA, something they have been working at for at least four years.

The clubs should control the A-League same as English teams run the Premier League. FFA should look after everything else, from the Socceroos to the W-League and so on.

We should not hold our collective breath about this happening anytime soon, though.

A prominent FFA official once told me that the governing body had little faith in most clubs' ability to properly run their own business, hence Oxford Street's reluctance to give them the reins.

Recent events would suggest that FFA's maestros are not exactly covering themselves in a blaze of glory by the way they are conducting the game.

They are very much out of tune with the game's needs.

A-League crowds are down, television ratings are depressing, there are very few genuine crowd-pulling stars and several clubs are in dire financial straits.

More importantly, the natives across the country are getting restless.

In other words, dark clouds are gathering over the league and this makes you wonder who in fact is squatting over a licence ... the clubs or the FFA.

These are very serious concerns as the A-League enters a second decade.

They certainly are hurdles that need to be overcome if club football is to continue to flourish in a tough and unforgiving sporting market.

But history teaches us that they are not insurmountable barriers and if everybody works together for a common cause the game will be much better for it.

The problem is the clubs do not trust the FFA anymore.

* * *

As the bitter row over the size of the FFA congress escalated into a full-scale war, the leadership of chairman Steven Lowy came under attack.

For the good of the game, Steven Lowy, just go
11 August 2017

Football Federation Australia have lost the plot, the dressing room and any semblance of goodwill they once shared with a frustrated football fraternity.

The board should do the right thing and step down.

Chairman Steven Lowy has done himself no favours with his antagonistic, arrogant and provocative approach towards the job he controversially inherited from his father Frank two years ago.

The governing body completed its latest public relations disaster with the abysmal handling of the row with the stakeholders over the size of its congress.

As if the arrival of FIFA and AFC officials to supervise meetings designed to sort out the colossal mess was not embarrassing enough—now the foreign representatives have departed our shores with the distinct feeling that our football is a complete basket case.

Regardless of who is right or wrong in one of the most bitter and damaging rows that have hit our game in decades, the FFA as football guardians in this country must shoulder most of the blame for the impasse that will have massive repercussions.

The FFA in one fell swoop have managed to achieve what others have failed to do for years: unite many of the game's stakeholders.

The only difference is that this time most of the football family is united in its dislike and mistrust of the governing body.

The football community also has lost faith in the modus operandi of its patronising administration that has been accused of treating its stakeholders as school children.

And when club chairmen openly call for the FFA board to resign and describe the FFA leadership as toxic, you know that the time has come for the game to change direction.

Even if a compromise—though highly unlikely at this stage—is reached by November, it is hard to imagine the game's stakeholders working together for the good of the game after what transpired in the last two weeks.

The damage caused by the recent shenanigans will have a lasting effect on our sport if the FFA is allowed to keep running it in its highly controversial style.

The FFA won't change and this is why it has to go. It's as simple as that.

Australian football has made great strides forward on many levels and to be fair we probably would not have a game to argue and bicker about were it not for the intervention of Frank Lowy more than a decade ago.

It all started so positively: Australia got out of the hole called Oceania to join Asia, the professional A-League was formed and the Socceroos qualified for the first of three straight FIFA World Cups with the healthy prospect of a fourth.

Things are different now, much different.

Hope that our game had finally cracked it in such a 'hostile' country as Australia has been replaced by frustration and a feeling of déjà vu.

Our faith in an administration that was obtaining positive results has made way for mistrust.

And our belief that we had reached a stage where we were working towards a common goal has transformed itself into indignation among the fans who as always are the ones to suffer most from this impasse.

And there is no point reiterating who is to blame for this abysmal state of affairs.

Lowy and his cohorts had an obligation and should have had the foresight to make sure the row never got to this stage but they failed miserably.

In 1987, as Sydney City president, Frank Lowy in a fit of pique famously 'picked up the ball and went home' and withdrew his battling club from the National Soccer League.

He was later accused of disrespect towards the game.

Steven Lowy should do the same and quit the game ... and take his board with him. Nobody would accuse him of disrespect.

*   *   *

The introduction of the video assistant referee in the A-League became a toxic topic of hot debate in Australia. It was not the success it was hoped to be.

Get rid of VAR, it's killing the A-League
17 December 2017

Enough is enough: Football Federation Australia for just once should listen to the fans and do us all a favour by ditching VAR.

Not in March when it is due for a review but now.

The system is destroying the image and credibility of the A-League and turning it into a circus and a joke.

The fans hate it, the players and coaches are confused, and quite frankly VAR is far more trouble than it is worth.

It is probably the cause for an alarming drop in crowd figures and television audiences this season.

'It's football but not as you know it' was the FFA's slogan when the competition kicked off in 2005.

It certainly is the case today because in one fell swoop the FFA has changed the game's fabric and managed to do what no one had ever done: unite the football family.

There are pockets of resistance to the clamour for giving the system a red card and a life ban.

Some claim there is nothing wrong with the concept except that it is badly managed.

Some maintain that the pursuit of fairness and justice on the field should be paramount in the debate.

Others say FFA is trying to improve poor refereeing standards that have blighted the A-League since day one and should be commended.

But these factors are not the main issues.

What matters most is that the fans who pay money to watch their sport hate it because it has robbed football of its spontaneity and human element.

It has become too much of a stop-start affair. Is this the kind of football we would like to see?

It also looks like the game today is refereed by somebody high up in the stands and on-field referees are reluctant to make the big decisions anymore. Why would they?

It makes you wonder if we need referees and their assistants anymore if everything is controlled from above or elsewhere.

VAR was supposed to intervene only on occasions when clear errors have been made by referees but it is not the case as was seen in the game between Central Coast and Western Sydney when two yellow cards were overturned and two home players were sent off, sparking howls of protest from coach Paul Okon and the spectators.

If FFA is smart it should ditch its attitude of 'we know what's best for football' and admit its experiment has been a colossal fiasco.

It should tell FIFA 'thanks but not thanks'.

FFA actually has no choice because as VAR becomes more farcical every week fewer and fewer fans will bother with the A-League anymore.

Eleven rounds into the competition have given us controversy upon controversy, which is unfortunate because we really should be talking about the pretty decent football the teams are providing this season ... most of the time, anyway. The number of 'golazos' we have seen this season is extraordinary.

Instead we are seeing in front of our own eyes a dramatic transformation and disintegration of the simple game we all grew to love.

Refereeing standards in Australia have always been low and the advent of professionalism has not improved matters greatly.

To be fair, coaches, players and fans have always complained about referees, particularly when they are on the losing end.

However, VAR has not reduced those complaints but increased them substantially ... so why change?

Clearly, VAR is not the answer and we should go back to where we were and accept the game, warts and all.

Football with all its faults and weaknesses is the world's most popular game and it has been doing rather well for itself for more than a century.

It does not need to change for the sake of being like other sports, thank you very much.

* * *

Season 2017–18 of the A-League reached a point where the need for a facelift was never more urgent. The clamour for a second division became louder by the day.

A-League is warned: populate or perish
3 March 2018

The A-League has reached a level of such sameness and inertia that Football Federation Australia has no other choice now but to give the club scene a facelift and set up a second division as soon as possible.

No ifs and buts. It is the only way to rejuvenate a stagnant competition that has become so stale despite a respectable playing standard that dissatisfied supporters across the board are up in arms and clamouring for change.

The vast majority of the game's stakeholders are tired of the competition that is gasping for fresh air and want a second division with consequent promotion and relegation. More so than the mooted expansion.

FFA has said it will consider the merits of expanding the A-League from 10 teams to 12 in the next two seasons but it has poured cold water on the demand for a second division from the football natives that are becoming more restless by the week.

Headquarters has given several reasons for its reluctance to make club football more representative of the wider football family's needs and aspirations. Unaffordability is one of them.

Yet the suspicion remains that FFA fears that it would be taking the game back to its 'dark old days' by inviting former National Soccer League clubs back into the fold in the form of a second division.

In its bid to appease an unforgiving and unsympathetic mainstream media, FFA has become paranoid about fans' misbehaviour and the bad publicity it generates and it will not gamble unnecessarily after 'cleaning up' the game's image.

A second division that includes promotion and relegation would add much-needed interest in the club scene, apart from giving aspiring footballers greater opportunities to show what they can do.

By the same token, I am not entirely convinced that the battling A-League is ready for promotion and relegation.

Getting the A-League's house in order should take prominence over such 'fanciful' ideas as a national second tier. First things first, right?

The problem, however, is the A-League is in serious trouble with falling crowds and audiences and it has no other alternative but to take a step forward and gamble in a bid to eliminate an alarming state of ennui that has gripped our game.

'Populate or perish' was a post-war political slogan that urged Australians to reconsider the country's attitude towards immigration.

It could easily be applied to the A-League because failure to do so could spell the end of the competition as we know it.

FFA, which is seen in some quarters as being more interested in its own survival than that of the game it is supposed to govern, has a massive responsibility.

Former chairman Frank Lowy did a great job of salvaging what was left of the old soccer and turning it into a new football; however, there is very little faith in the current leadership across the football community.

Frank's son Steven, who took over the chairmanship in controversial circumstances, in a short time has alienated himself to most of the game's stakeholders while CEO David Gallop's popularity continues to plummet.

The clubs are unhappy with several issues, many disillusioned players can't wait to move anywhere abroad, the frustrated fans have been made to feel irrelevant and, last but not least, main broadcasters Foxtel are getting very nervous about a declining product they have paid considerable money for the privilege of showing.

If Steven Lowy really loves the game, he and his maligned board have to do something pretty fast to save it from terminal decline.

And one way to appease the exasperated clubs, the disgruntled fans and the disillusioned media is to give them what they want: a second division with promotion and relegation.

FFA says it cannot afford it. Many would say FFA cannot afford not to.

* * *

The FFA's unpopular national club identity policy came under renewed attack after a regional team was forced to change their 'ethnic' name.

FFA's mistaken identity policy faces a challenge
30 August 2018

True lovers of Australian football are hoping that a little known club from northern NSW wins a legal battle with Football Federation Australia over its right to call itself what it wants.

Charlestown City Blues, who play in the Northern NSW premier league, have challenged the governing body after they were ordered to change their original name Azzurri.

The Italian-backed club has taken its case to the Australian Human Rights Commission, the *Newcastle Herald* reported.

And if need be, the Blues—that's English for Azzurri—are adamant they would go to the Supreme Court in a bid to have their name reinstated.

The FFA edict is all part of the unpopular National Club Identity Policy, which was launched in 2014 in a highly controversial move to eliminate ethic, national, political, religious and racial links to all clubs' names, logos and emblems.

FFA Cup quarter-finalists Avondale were ordered to hide a little Italian flag at the back of their jerseys before their round of 32 tie with Marconi, prompting widespread calls for the "ridiculous" policy to be scrapped.

The move was designed to rid the Australian game of its perceived 'foreignness' as it sought to amalgamate with mainstream Australian sport in a simpler and more recognisable way.

Which was all well and good at the time but the policy has gone too far.

I have no problem with the FFA trying to stamp out the 'ethnic' nature of our old game which occasionally gave ordinary matches an ulterior edge that could have caused outbreaks of crowd disturbances.

And I understand that by aligning themselves to foreign entities via their names or badges, clubs would appeal to only a limited section of society, thereby restricting their fan bases and marketing and sponsorship capacity.

Not just of the clubs themselves but also of the league they played in.

But if we look at things objectively, we should ask ourselves how on earth can any club—particularly in such a multicultural country as Australia—be told to change their name because it sounds too foreign?

Especially if a club happens to be an old, established organisation founded against all the odds by migrants and see their name as the emblem of their history and tradition.

What's wrong with AC Milan, who were founded by an English group in 1899, calling themselves 'Mee-lan' instead of the Italian 'Milano'?

Brazil's Vasco da Gama owe their name to the famous explorer and to a set of Portuguese football lovers who launched the club in 1898.

River Plate of Argentina prefer to be called so instead of the more Hispanic 'Rio Plata'.

As far as I know nobody in Italy, Brazil or Argentina complains about this glaring foreign element in their midst.

It is also worth mentioning that our own governing body changed its name from Soccer Australia to Football Federation of Australia at the turn of the century when it became obvious that the latter would suit them much better.

Nobody from outside our game would even dare complain about this because the FFA quite rightly would tell anybody brave or foolish enough to do so to go jump in the river.

A-League and NPL clubs should also be afforded this sacrosanct right.

Club officials are not stupid and they would not rush into things without proper consideration.

And if they do make a wrong decision they would be the ones to suffer the consequences.

Essentially because what they call themselves is their decision and not FFA's.

The FFA could do much worse than reconsider its stance on the identity of the clubs.

* * *

'QUOTE UNQUOTE'

The COVID-19 pandemic that caused havoc around the world could be a blessing in disguise for Australia and New Zealand in their joint bid to hold the Women's World Cup.

Pandemic could land Matildas a home World Cup
16 May 2020

The expertise of Australia and New Zealand in dealing efficiently with the threat of COVID-19 should serve the two countries in good stead when FIFA delivers its verdict on hosting rights for the 2023 Women's World Cup.

Australia and New Zealand have forged a strong alliance in a bid to jointly stage the blue-riband event of women's football in three years.

The other bidders are Brazil, Colombia and Japan.

"Our world-class infrastructure, modern stadia, high-quality football facilities in Australia and New Zealand and major event-hosting experience ensure certainty in delivering the first 32-team World Cup," Football Federation Australia chairman Chris Nikou said.

"From operational excellence, record-breaking crowds, commercial success, strong government support, a warm embrace from our 200 diverse cultures to a genuine profound legacy across the Asia-Pacific region, Australia-New Zealand offers certainty in uncertain times, as well as impact."

FIFA has announced that its 37-member council will make its final decision on June 25 and the voting process will be made public online.

"FIFA has today confirmed to the bidding member associations that the selection of the host(s) of the FIFA Women's World Cup 2023 by the FIFA Council will be made at its meeting to be held online on June 25," a statement read.

FFA would be confident that federal government's ability to deal competently and effectively with whatever crises—such as the coronavirus—come our way may have created a perception among voters of a country that is perfectly capable of hosting such a big event.

Our federal and state governments are leading the way and cooperating, our health system works efficiently, our public order is reliable and our economic drag won't last as long as those in Brazil, Colombia and Japan which are more deeply affected by the pandemic.

Now that Australia is gingerly but surely moving out of its most difficult period we could be seen as not only FIFA's most reliable partners but also the most exciting because a World Cup in the Antipodes would be the first time women's biggest tournament would be played in two countries and across two confederations.

If Australia and New Zealand land the big prize in little over a month, the popular Matildas would never get a better chance of winning the one trophy that has eluded them.

The tournament will be held in July and August.

About the Author

Philip Micallef is a retired sports journalist who has worked full time for Fairfax (Illawarra Mercury) and News Ltd (Daily Telegraph and Sunday Telegraph). He also was a long-time contributor to SBS (The World Game). He has vast experience in the production side of newspapers and websites as well as a reporter and opinion writer.

He has covered many major football events such as the World Cup, the European Championships, the Copa America, the UEFA and AFC Champions League tournaments plus dozens of Socceroos, National Soccer League and A-League matches.

He also has interviewed enough top footballers to be able to compile a strong 'World XI'. He is the author of 'The World Cup Story, An Australian View' that was published in 1994.

Philip, who was born in Malta, migrated to Australia in 1981 and lives in Sydney. His two favourite teams are the Socceroos and AC Milan.

Really good football books

Code War$
The Battle for Fans, Dollars and Survival
by Dr Hunter Fujak

The Itinerant Coach
by Steve Darby

The Away Game
by Matthew Hall

Achieving the Impossible
- the Remarkable Story of How Greece Won EURO 2004
by George Tsitsonis

Riding Shotgun
by Andy Bernal

Surfing for England
Our Lost Socceroos
by Jason Goldsmith

100 Years of Football at Wynnum
by Vicky Krayem

Encyclopedia of Matildas
Revised and Updated
by Andrew Howe
and Greg Werner

Encyclopedia of Socceroos
by Andrew Howe

'If I Started to Cry, I Wouldn't Stop' by Matthew Hall

The A-Z of Socceroos - World Cup Edition 2018 by Andrew Howe (with Ray Gatt and Bonita Mersiades)

Playing for Australia The First Socceroos, Asia and the World Game by Trevor Thompson

Dedicated Lives by Greg Downes

The World Cup Chronicles 31 Days that Rocked Brazil by Jorge Knijnik

Chronicles of Soccer in Australia - The Foundation Years 1859 to 1949 by Peter Kunz

The Aboriginal Soccer Tribe by John Maynard

Support Your Local League, A South-East Asian Football Odyssey by Antony Sutton

If I Started to Cry Matthew Hall

Be My Guest by Jason Goldsmith and Lucas Gillard

Available from

fairplaypublishing.com.au

and all

good bookstores

Jarrod Black Guilty Party by Texi Smith (Popcorn Press)

Achieving the Impossible - the Remarkable Story of How Greece Won EURO 2004 by George Tsitsonis

www.fairplaypublishing.com.au

www.ingramcontent.com/pod-product-compliance
Lightning Source LLC
Chambersburg PA
CBHW071731080526
44588CB00013B/1984